LIGHTENING
YOUR
LOAD

Repacking
Your Bags for
a Fuller Life

NANCY EICHMAN
21st Century Christian Publishing

ISBN: 978-0-89098-923-4

©2016 by 21st Century Christian

2809 12th Ave S, Nashville, TN 37204

All rights reserved.

Unless otherwise noted Scripture quotations are from the English Standard Version.

Scripture quotations are from The Holy Bible, English Standard Version® (ESV®),

copyright © 2001 by Crossway, a publishing ministry of Good News Publishers.

Used by permission. All rights reserved.

Unless otherwise noted Scripture quotations are from the New King James Version.

Scripture taken from the New King James Version.

Copyright © 1982 by Thomas Nelson, Inc. Used by permission. All rights reserved.

Cover design by Jonathan Edelhuber

TABLE OF CONTENTS

DEDICATION

To my precious grandson ~ Isaac White

Your name means "laughter"
and your smiles and laughter lighten my load.

To my dear family ~
Phil Eichman, John Eichman, Phil and Amy White

Thanks for lightening my load
with your support and encouragement.

WHAT TO PACK

Author Charles Dudley Warner once said, "Simplicity is making the journey of this life with just baggage enough." Packing just enough can be a real challenge. Often in our hurry to pack for life, we forget something important. Although some items are not necessities, others are crucial. In the following chapters are some things we shouldn't miss putting on our packing lists.

PACKING LIGHT?

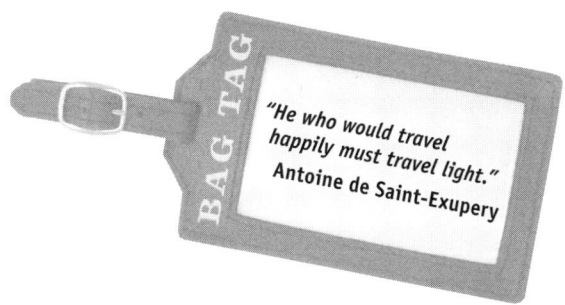

BAG TAG

"He who would travel happily must travel light." Antoine de Saint-Exupery

H and me a bag, and I'll soon be packing to travel. Well, make that several bags. I always seem to pack too much stuff. I believe in being prepared to the extreme. I load up my bags to prepare for the "what ifs," "maybes," and "just in cases" of the trip. If I need clothes for a week, I'll throw in some extra in case of a tornado or hurricane. I mustn't forget a book to read—wait, what if I finish that one? I'll pitch in three more. Oh, and how about shoes—can you ever have enough shoes?

In my vocabulary, "pack" and "light" don't belong in the same sentence!

Unfortunately, my overpacking doesn't stop there. I've found that I also pack my life with too much stuff. My schedule is crammed with multiple to-do lists. Multitasking mania consumes me. My cabinets, closets, and garage are full of stuff, yet I buy more. Unhealthy habits like procrastination and discontentment clutter my life.

This clutter spills over into my spiritual life and crowds out God. Instead of looking to Him to take care of me, I burden myself with worry and overwork in an attempt to take care of any eventuality on my own. I lose my focus on what is important and get distracted from spiritual things. I become overextended, overwrought, and overwhelmed.

Are you like me? Are you going through life encumbered with excess baggage? Do you ever ask yourself, *How can I take on one more thing?*

Life is hard enough without burdening ourselves with more than we need. Overpacking our lives can be exhausting and exasperating. It can trip us up. It can even bury us in an early grave!

As we travel through life, it's too easy to pack more than we need. But Jesus offers us an alternative to our overpacked lives. He invites us to take on a fuller life with a lighter load. How can we pack "fuller" yet "lighter"? Such a paradox leads us to an exhilarating discovery of how to live a better way. Though each of us must carry her own burden, the Lord has promised to be with us and lighten our load. In fact, He offers us relief from our spiritual exhaustion—rest for our souls! I'm ready to learn how to lighten my load. Are you?

CHAPTER 1

ENOUGH!
Discovering the Upside of Downsizing

"You can't have everything— where would you put it?"
Steven Wright

What would it be like if you owned just the clothes on your back? You lived from one day to the next? You welcomed an invitation to visit friends because you didn't have a home of your own?

Sounds like you would be a homeless person, right? It's actually a description of Jesus. Christ doesn't call us to be homeless with only one set of clothes. But He does exemplify for us a simpler lifestyle, a life void of excess and pretense.

Someone might think, *Sure, it would be easy for him. He didn't live in the complicated, stress-infested society we experience today.* It's true that on earth Jesus didn't face smog-filled rush hour traffic, mind-boggling technology overload, and heart-breaking mass shootings. But he did encounter dysfunctional families, rampant crime, and political upheaval in the Middle East. He knew the ever-present dichotomy of the powerless versus the powerful. He observed firsthand the chaos in people's lives when they didn't know God. He saw their wasted lives from a lack of purpose and peace. He sought to offer a better alternative.

LIFESTYLES OF THE RICH AND HOARDING

When Jesus came to earth, His life and teaching showed us what was really important. He told one story about a man who thought he was ready to live it up. This rich farmer had grown such an abundant crop that he made grandiose plans of tearing down his old barns and building bigger ones, just to hold his bumper crop and goods. His future looked bright for years to come and an easy "eat, drink, and be merry" lifestyle was within his grasp. However, that night he died and God demanded an account of his greedy life that stored up things for himself but not toward God (Luke 12:16-21). The rich fool had an opportunity to share his wealth with God and others. Instead, he hoarded it for himself. In the end, he never was able to enjoy his newfound riches. He totally misunderstood where his priorities should have lain.

Is Jesus teaching in this parable that we should not store anything for the future? Proverbs 21:20 specifically points to the wisdom of storing goods in preparing for the future: "The wise store up choice food and olive oil, but fools gulp theirs down." Likewise, ants are praised for being extremely wise for storing up their food in the summer (Proverbs 30:24-25). Through God's direction, Joseph stored grain in Egypt in preparation for the seven years of famine (Genesis 41:46-57). The five wise virgins exemplified farsighted thinking by storing extra oil so that they would be ready to meet the bridegroom (Matthew 25:1-13).

What then was the Lord condemning in the rich fool? If we closely examine the rich fool's thinking, we see he focused on what *he* would do with *his* barns, grain, and goods. He never saw beyond himself or his world. It is not wrong to be rich or to store things for the future. Rather, it is wrong to store things only for ourselves and forget about God and others.

SQUIRRELING STUFF AWAY

Jesus' story is as timely today as it was then. Though we might not hoard in the same way as the rich fool in Jesus' parable, we need to examine why we buy and keep stuff. Do we have tendencies to buy more stuff than we will ever use? When we have been blessed, are we more likely to stockpile the surplus instead of sharing with others? Do we hoard things because we do not trust in God to provide? Let's meet some ladies who go nuts squirreling stuff away.

Hideaway Heidi has this thing for shoes and can't stop buying them. In her mind, the shoes make the outfit. She's running out of innovative ways to hide her new purchases from her husband, who has said they can't afford any more.

Resale Renee bargain shops at consignment boutiques so her wardrobe is less expensive than it would be at regular cost. She "makes up the difference" by buying more clothes. Now her closet is so full she can't find a thing to wear.

Online Olivia is a computer-shopping junkie who is proud of all the money she saves with online deals. When a purchase don't work out, she hates the hassle of returning them, so she just stashes them.

Bargain Betty can sniff out grocery bargains all over town. Her dilemma comes when she gets home and finds she already has so many of the same things in the pantry that she will never use them all before the expiration dates.

Collectible Colleen's collection of novelty pigs is taking over her house. She buys one wherever she sees one she doesn't own, and her friends keep giving her more. Her husband has started dreaming about attack oinkers.

These ladies definitely have problems with buying and storing stuff. It is easy to think that bringing one more thing home won't make a difference, but sometimes we have to say, "Enough! No more!" When we head for the store, flea market, or website and find something we want, let's be intentional and ask these questions:

- Why do I want this?
- How many do I already have?
- Do I have somewhere to put it?
- Do I really need one (or two or five or ten)?

DIAGNOSIS: WE HAVE "STUFFITIS"

Americans are infected with a clear case of "stuffitis," the malady of owning too much stuff. A UCLA study reported that Los Angeles middle class families are "battling a nearly universal overaccumulation of goods."[1] Sociologist Juliet Schor reported that the average consumer in America buys a new piece of clothing every five and a half days. That seems extreme but a look in our closets makes us wonder.[2]

While reality TV viewers see people who go to extremes of hoarding, its various forms can also touch our lives because we are so materially blessed. For example, just take America's dependence on self-storage units that dot our landscape. These units were originally intended for those in transition (moving, divorcing, or settling an estate), but now people use them who don't have enough room for their stuff at home. A 2007 Self-Storage Association study found that 50 percent of customers use these units for their extra belongings, even though the average size of an American home has doubled in the last 50 years. Many of these units are used for stuff people don't want or need.[3]

For many people, self-storage units have become the "bigger barns" of Jesus' parable. The Lord reminds us that our treasures on earth can get moth-eaten, corroded, and stolen in temporary storage units and any other earthly place. For eternal things that are really important, it's much better to use the only sure and safe storage unit—heaven (Matthew 6:19-21).

DON'T OPEN THAT DOOR!

Let's face it—if we can't find something after a search requiring an archeological dig, it's lost to us, and we don't have it. Often we can't locate what we own because of our clutter. Nowhere is this more evident than in our garages, attics, and basements, the "no man's land" of our homes. Our motto is, "Don't open that door." We are ashamed of what people will think, muddled on how to keep the stuff corralled, and afraid of falling debris. As an unknown wit once observed, "Only in America do we leave cars worth thousands of dollars in the driveway and put our useless junk in the garage."

To avoid "open door shame," send the packrat packing by embracing these broad decluttering strategies:

Weed the excess so you own less. Make a schedule (consider 12 weeks as a possible goal with two-hour sessions on a timer). Go through your home with three heavy-duty bags deciding what to toss, donate, and decide on later. Ask yourself if you have used it in the last year. Be decisive and move quickly.[4]

Everything needs a space to put it in its place. Store what you have efficiently, attractively, and when possible, out of sight. For example, in the garage, map out and designate centers on paper first (think sports, tool, yard/garden, recycling, activity, and car care centers). Then put like items on the wall, ceiling, and shelves with labeled boxes and see-through containers.

Put it back—don't spread or stack. When you see a pile of stuff, it represents deferred decisions. Someone decided not to put each item back in its place. So break the cycle, take the few extra minutes, and put the item back or in a basket to return to later when you can. Flat areas are clutter magnets, so don't put it down; put it back.

John Ruskin, Victorian social critic, once said, "Every increased possession loads us with a new weariness." Think about it: Every purchase we make may need to be washed, ironed, dry cleaned, insured, waxed, polished, maintained, updated, secured, dusted, vacuumed—and that's only the beginning. All these added together demand more of our money, time, space, and energy. It fills up our lives with more stuff to do and remember. It is easy to see how more stuff complicates our lives exponentially.

So is more really better? Do we have to own the best or can it be good enough? Do we have to possess the biggest or can it be big enough? Do we have to have the most or can we have just enough?

A FULLER, YET LIGHTER LOAD

What if we could find fullness in life that wasn't based on accumulating stuff? Jesus said, "...I came that they may have life and have it abundantly" (John 10:10). The Greek word for the expression "abundantly" means "over and above, more than enough superabundance."[5] We know that an eternal life in heaven will be beyond our wildest dreams. But Jesus also offers us a superabundant life now full of joy, power, and fellowship with God. This means that we can enjoy a life "over the top" without materialistic trappings and pitfalls. Jesus turns the world's mantra that "bigger is better" upside down with revolutionary, paradoxical ideas like these:

- Less is more (Matthew 6:19-21).

- Giving can bring abundant returns (Acts 20:35).

- Just enough can be more than enough (Matthew 6:33-34).

Along with this superabundant life, Jesus also offers relief from crushing burdens like crippling anxiety, a guilty conscience, and a sense of futility and frustration. Instead of the heavy baggage we pack and lug around by trying to do things on our own, Jesus offers a lighter alternative to our overloaded lives:

> "Come to me, all you who labor and are heavy laden, and I will give you rest. Take my yoke upon you and learn from me, for I am gentle and lowly in heart, and you will find rest for your souls. For my yoke is easy and my burden is light" (Matthew 11:28-30).

Only Jesus can offer a fuller, yet lighter load. He can give us rest and peace the world can't provide if we follow Him, take on His yoke, and learn from His teaching (John 14:27). His yoke is not like the cumbersome load of the Pharisees, who tried to obey hundreds of man-made rules and regulations (Matthew 23:1-4). Rather, the path of Jesus ultimately offers a lighter load because our obedience is based on love (1 John 5:3-4).

The commentator William Barclay tells of a legend that Jesus had a carpenter shop in Nazareth with a sign outside that read "My yokes fit well." According to the legend, customers would come to the shop from all over the country because Jesus was known for carving well-fitting yokes for their animals.[6] While we don't know if this legend is true, we do know that in Matthew 11:30, the Greek work for "easy" means "good, gentle, easy to use or bear...having nothing harsh or galling about it."[7] Perhaps Jesus was using this image of a yoke to show that the life He offers is not a burden to break us under its load, but is measured to fit us well. As Barclay explains, "Whatever God sends us is made to fit our needs and our abilities exactly...The burden which is given in love and carried in love is always light."[8]

So Jesus is not calling us to a life of careless ease or painful drudgery. Rather, He invites us to live a full life of joy in which we empty ourselves to others. We can know true rest and peace by wearing the yoke of Christ. We can delight in our lighter load, for it is one we can gladly bear. For what is lighter than a burden that can actually unburden us? Where else can we take on a yoke that gives us rest?

ARE WE THERE YET?

1. Why do you think Jesus chose to live such a simple lifestyle on earth? What are some ways we could live a simpler lifestyle so that others could simply live?

2. What is the difference between hoarding and storing? What are some different ways we can hoard our blessings?

3. Why did Jesus condemn the rich farmer? How is his "eat, drink, and be merry" philosophy lived out today in our world?

4. In another of Jesus' parables, who else was rich and self-absorbed with no thoughts of the poor (Luke 16:19-31)? How does Matthew 16:26 apply to him?

5. In this chapter, what were some problems of the five women who stored stuff? How do you think they could solve these problems?

6. Why is it important to stop and think before making purchases? Why is this especially difficult in today's consumer culture?

7. Why are we so prone to "stuffitis"? How does accumulating more stuff add to our already burdened lives?

8. What are three broad strategies we can use to declutter our homes and lives?

9. How do the blessings of the superabundant life in Christ contrast with what people consider as "the good life" today?

10. What are some paradoxes in Jesus' invitation in Matthew 11:28-30?

TRIP TIPS: Preventing "Stuffitis"

To prepare for the worldwide famine, Joseph filled the Egyptian storehouses with so much grain "that he stopped keeping records because it was beyond measure" (Genesis 41:49). Before your possessions mushroom "beyond measure," it's time to cut the clutter to prevent "stuffitis."

Chasing Paper ~ Drowning in information? To stay afloat in the sea of paper in our lives, use the RAFT method (Refer, Action, File or Toss) of mail sorting. If it's junk mail, toss it in the recycling bin or trash right after you pick up your mail. Otherwise, refer it to someone who can act on it, act on it yourself, or file it for future reference. [9]

Saving Trees ~ Magazines, newspapers, and catalogs accumulate in no time. "Rip and read" it, file it, and then recycle the rest or pass it on to others to enjoy. If you must save a whole catalog, file only the most recent and weed the rest. Better still, read and order online to save paper and trees. Whether or not you are reading more digital or paper books, take a look at your bookshelf. Will you really read all the books there or could you donate some of them to a library or charitable organization? You can also order many titles from your public library through interlibrary loan.

Remembering Aunt Susie ~ Sometimes a gift's value lies in its sentimental connection of the giver to us. Treasure the gift if your memories of it are precious. But don't feel obligated to keep something just because a relative used/loved/valued it. Instead value the precious memories you have of the person because they will last longer.

BAGGAGE CLAIM

"One cannot collect all the beautiful shells on the beach. One can only collect a few, and they are more beautiful if they are few." Anne Morrow Lindberg

"It all depends on whether you have things, or they have you." Robert A. Cook

"My motto is 'enough' not only for me but that all people would have enough to have a good life. 'Enough' has an upper as well as a lower threshold." Claire Mayer

"God prospers me not to raise my standard of living, but to raise my standard of giving." Randy Alcorn

"God is always trying to give good things to us, but our hands are too full to receive them." Augustine

BRING IT ON HOME

What one thing can you do this week to lighten your load by packing some simplicity in your life? Write it here:

CHAPTER 2

ORDER
Managing Some Method in Our Madness

"I got it all together but forgot where I put it!"

Unknown

P acking up and traveling in a foreign country is always an adventure. This was especially true in Guatemala City, where our mission team landed one summer. After our bags were loaded on the roof of the bus, we set off in city traffic. There were no chickens on our "chicken bus" unless you counted those of us who feared for our lives. Drivers dared to play "every man for himself" as vehicles weaved in and out, ignoring traffic lights and merging where others feared to tread. It was a perfect picture of disorder.

Whether we are traveling on the road or through life, disorder can be chaotic and upsetting while order can breed peace and consistency. One day in the life of Jesus exemplifies this very dichotomy.

ORDERING DINNER FOR A CROWD

Anyone who has ever fed a crowd knows how chaotic it can be. Now imagine what it would be like to cater to 5,000 hungry people in the middle of nowhere. What would you pack for a trip like that? How would you transport the food, the tables, and the personnel to serve the food? How could you keep such a task from becoming pandemonium *ala carte*? Even in today's world, such a proposal would be an intimidating feat. But Jesus handled the same daunting challenge with ease.

It might have become an unsettling situation. In a remote place, more than 5,000 men, women, and children were thronging to see Jesus teach and heal (Matthew 14:21). Some even ran to find a spot (Mark 6:33). Evening was coming, and the people were getting hungry. This presented a real dilemma. Should the crowd be sent away? If not, how could such a great crowd be fed?

Jesus and His disciples discussed solutions to the problem, but none of the disciples' ideas seemed plausible. Spending more than eight month's salary to feed everyone seemed unreasonable but so did dividing a small boy's five barley loaves and two fish (John 6:7-8). Jesus knew what He was going to do, so He started to give instructions.

Jesus directed the disciples to have the crowds sit down in groups of fifties and hundreds (Mark 6:39-40). Since it was spring-time near the feast of Passover, there was green grass in the area. After Jesus gave thanks for the five barley loaves and two fishes, they were distributed to the people. Everyone was fed and filled from the same loaves and fishes. The disciples even collected 12 baskets of leftover broken pieces (Luke 9:16-17).

To feed so many people with so little and then to end up with more than they started—there could be no doubt that Jesus performed this awesome miracle through the power of God. This was evident to the people who said, "Surely this is the prophet who is to come into the world" (John 6:14). They referred to Moses' prophecy that God would raise up a prophet like him (Deuteronomy 18:15, 18-19). The people planned to force Jesus to become their king. Knowing their thoughts, Jesus dismissed the crowds and withdrew by Himself to a mountain to pray. They did not understand that Jesus was indeed their king, but His kingdom was not of this world (John 18:36).

TOWARD A GREATER PURPOSE

What was the purpose of this extraordinary dinner on the grounds? It was to demonstrate that Jesus was God's Son, the

Messiah. Some people realized this great truth while others only sought to fill their stomachs (John 6:26). It was Jesus' intention to glorify God in this way as "he himself knew what he would do" (John 6:6). Jesus could have done this in any way He chose because His Father's power was infinite, but He chose an orderly process to accomplish it.

Miraculously feeding 5,000 plus people is beyond our power. We cannot accomplish what Jesus did that day. However, we can emulate the principles He used in the details.

To organize the distribution of food, first the people were seated on the grass. Then they were divided into groups of 50 and 100. This could have served as a visual count of the people to show the magnitude of the miracle. It also made the distribution of food more manageable, which at best was time-consuming for at least 100 groups of 50. After the crowds had eaten all they wanted, the scraps of bread were collected in twelve baskets. Jesus could have left the scraps, but instead they were gathered and not wasted. The leftovers served as tangible evidence of the miracle and reminded them of His power.

It is striking that Jesus chose an orderly process to accomplish His purpose. He serves as an example to us in our hectic lives to utilize order. After all, Jesus is like His Father, who is the God of order.

PEACE AND ORDER ARE IN GOD'S NATURE

Paul gives us insight into the nature of God in 1 Corinthians 14:33: "For God is not a God of confusion but of peace." Order is in God's nature. God created the heavens and the earth in a deliberate sequence and logical order. He made a habitat for living things in His world, then created plants and animals, and finally formed human beings to rule over and care for it all (Genesis 1:26).

God also gave His people detailed laws, first through Moses and then later through Christ. God specified orderly worship first in the tabernacle, then the temple, and finally the assemblies of the church (1 Corinthians 14:40).

Because God is an orderly God, He knew how disorder could cause havoc. At times He used disorder to confuse and confound those who did not obey Him. Take, for example, the builders who sought to build the Tower of Babel to the sky and make a name for themselves. God confused their language, so they were scattered all over the earth (Genesis 11:1-9). Remember also the panic-stricken Midianites who turned on each other with their swords when Gideon and his three hundred "dog-lapping" soldiers surrounded their camp with jars and trumpets (Judges 7:7-25). These examples just show how serious and disorienting the effects of disorder can be.

When we understand the benefits of God's orderly nature, we can see how order can bring consistency and peace to His creatures. When our lives have some semblance of order, we know what to expect. Order breeds a sense of harmony. It engenders peace of mind. It avoids confusion. Order and organization help us ultimately lighten our loads.

WHY WE NEED ORDER

In her book by the same title, Marilyn Paul makes the point, "It's hard to make a difference if you can't find your keys."[1] She emphasizes that often we miss opportunities, lose valuable time, and grow frustrated because of our disorganization. Think about it—have these things ever happened to you?

- You tell people you will pray for them, and then it slips your mind.
- You hardly ever make time to do things you would like to do.
- You are often late for Bible class, appointments, and meetings at work.
- You lose important memos, bills, or receipts.
- You start Bible study plans, but rarely finish them.

If these have ever happened to you, you are not alone. A National Association of Professional Organizers survey found that 96 percent of the respondents felt they could save time if they were more organized, with 71 percent indicating their quality of life would improve. It has been estimated that workers spend half their time searching for information because it was not organized properly.[2]

We can relate to this when we can't find that warranty for the new vacuum cleaner that just went kaput. Hit-or-miss living saps our energy. It can be exhausting and exasperating. It can even discourage and sabotage us in our walk with God. It is difficult to have peace in our hearts when our home life is chaotic. Some order in our lives can help us take care of life's routine details so we can accomplish the more important tasks that God calls us to do.

WAYS TO ORDER OUR LIVES

Although an orderly life has many benefits, it can be overwhelming to know where to begin. Professional organizer Kathy Waddill has simplified the process by defining simple habits she calls the "Nine Strategies of Reasonably Organized People." Check them out, to see if you could put something into practice that might lighten your load.

1. *"Make your systems fit you and your life."* You have to find what methods work for you, not someone else.

2. *"Sort everything by how you use it."* Keep similar items together to know how much you have and then put them where you use them.

3. *"Weed constantly."* When you keep what you don't use, it gets in the way.

4. *"Use the right containers and tools."* Ineffective tools and containers are hard to use and make more work for you.

5. *"Label everything."* Labeling things at first is usually faster than trying to figure out what is inside every time.

6. *"Keep it simple."* Learn to do your work efficiently so you will have more time for important things and people.

7. *"Decide to decide."* Indecision and procrastination hold you back and waste valuable time.

8. *"Get help when you need it."* Whether it is asking your family, friends, or an expert, don't be afraid to ask.

9. *"Evaluate honestly and often."* Your life is constantly changing and what worked before might not work now. [3]

ORGANIZATION IS PERSONAL

Organization is a personal thing. Some people want or need more order than others. Your sense of peace and order will be different from someone else's.

The challenge is to find the amount of organization in your life so it can run smoothly. There is no organization police saying you have to alphabetize your spices!

Spend some time evaluating what is important in your life. What would help you be closer to God and others? For example, do you feel housework is an overwhelming burden, preventing you from spending time with your family? Is there something in your schedule you could change? Could you delegate more responsibility to family members? Could you hire someone to help? How about doubling up meals and trading dinners with a friend once a week?

It's heartening to know you can start small, like organizing a drawer, cabinet, or even the car. Once you see how good it makes you feel, you will be ready to tackle something bigger. Having some control over your life helps you better handle the uncontrollable parts of life. Choose what matters most to you and spend a certain amount of time each week toward a smoother life. You will be surprised at what you can accomplish, and you will begin to feel more confident. Someone once said, "For every minute spent organizing, an hour is earned."

Many women think that getting organized will stifle their creativity and spontaneity—a kind of rigid straitjacket of "shoulds." In reality, it can be liberating. If your life is more organized, you will eventually find more time and money to do your artsy, spur-of-the-moment stuff. For example, if your bills are paid on time, you can take the money that you used to spend on late fees and put that toward a new canvas or weekend at the beach.

Reward yourself when you make progress. It can be challenging to maintain order after you have achieved it. When you streamline your closet, for instance, don't hang all same color clothes together unless you know you will continue to do it. It might be easier to maintain a simpler system like keeping types of clothes together like skirts, pants, and tops. Then again, it might be a real accomplishment just to hang the clothes in the closet and keep your "floordrobe" off the floor.

ORGANIZATION IS WORTH IT

Start with the areas of your life, home, and work that frustrate you the most. Think about what needs to change. Pray for guidance, asking God to help you develop more self-control and discipline in your life (Galatians 5:22-23). Read books and articles about the subject. Ask other women who seem to be organized what works for them. Try some different ideas. If something doesn't work, keep trying to find something that works for you. Find ways to manage life's details well so you can devote your time and energy to the more important people and things in your life—and to God. You will find less stress and more joy. By repacking your life with more order, you can lighten your load and find a more peaceful life.

Albert Einstein, the brilliant scientist, had wise advice for our lives: "Out of clutter, find simplicity. From discord, find harmony. In the middle of difficulty lies opportunity." It can start with organizing that first drawer.

ARE WE THERE YET?

1. What was the dilemma in this chapter that Jesus, His disciples, and the crowds faced? Why were the disciples' solutions not feasible?

2. What were some ways that order avoided confusion in feeding the crowd? How did it serve a greater purpose in Jesus' miracle?

3. Why might the people in the crowd compare Jesus with Moses (Exodus 16; Deuteronomy 18:15, 18; Acts 3:17-23)?

4. Why did some people want to force Jesus to become their king? Why did He leave instead (John 6:14-15)?

5. In what ways does God demonstrate that He is a God of peace and order? How did God, at times, use disorder to confuse and confound those who did not obey Him (Genesis 11:1-9; Judges 7:7-25)?

6. How can an unordered life affect us physically and sabotage us in our walk with God?

7. Why is it important to ask for help when we need it?

8. In what ways can getting organized eventually be liberating?

9. How do self-control and discipline play a part in an ordered life?

10. How can a more ordered life ultimately allow you to spend more time with God, your family, and your friends?

TRIP TIPS: Keeping on Track with Calendars

Have you ever felt your life was scattered all over the place? Calendars can help tie the loose ends of your life together. Some women prefer their mobile device or phone while others like a purse-size paper one. Any kind of portable personal calendar makes it easier to record your prayer requests, appointments, and lunches out with a friend.

To keep up with appointments, lessons, and sports, many households use a family calendar, a kind of "Family Central." If everyone in your family has a smartphone, they can connect with a calendar app. For some families, a paper calendar is more user-friendly because it can be big, visible, and accessible to all. Whichever is used, every family member old enough can be responsible for checking and listing his activities. Be sure that your family birthdays and necessary phone numbers are transferred to the calendar as well.

A prayer calendar can help you "pray without ceasing" (1 Thessalonians 5:17). By listing specific requests, you can pray for a variety of needs, especially when people ask you. There are a number of printed monthly calendars tailored to fit a Christian's general needs, complete with Scriptures. You could adopt such a calendar to your own situation. For example, you could remember church prayer requests on Sunday, family needs during the week, and other specific needs on Saturday.

Encourage your children to use their own phones or planners to record their assignments, practices, church outings, and school events. This can foster independence and accountability in their busy lives, just as it does in yours.

BAGGAGE CLAIM

"One person's mess is merely another person's filing system."
Margo Kaufman

"First comes thought; then organization of that thought, into ideas and plans; then transformation of those plans into reality. The beginning, as you will observe, is in your imagination."
Napoleon Hill

"Discipline is doing what needs to be done, when it needs to be done, when we don't want to do it." Bobbi DePorter

"Sometimes it takes more time to put something on your to-do list than it takes to just do it." Kathy Waddill

"No matter how big and tough a problem may be, get rid of confusion by taking one little step toward solution. Do something."
George F. Nordenholt

"You make the beds, you do the dishes, and six months later you have to start all over again." Joan Rivers

BRING IT ON HOME

What one thing can you do this week to lighten your load by packing more order into your life? Write it here:

_____

28

GRACE
Putting a Face on Grace

BAG TAG

"Grace isn't a little prayer you chant before receiving a meal. It's a way to live."
Jacqueline Winspear

The appeal is undeniable. The sense of adventure that often lures you to pack up your bags and leave the comforts of home is the exciting unknown—new places, new people, new experiences. However, the unknown can also bring you unforeseen problems like the motel desk clerk who set the 5:00 a.m. wakeup call for the wrong room—your room! Then there was that eagerly anticipated holiday getaway with the patriotic neighbors at your campsite who set off fireworks all evening, frightening the wildlife and raising your blood pressure. How about the airline check-in clerk who routed your luggage to BAE (France) instead of BAF (Massachusetts)?

So whether we cross the continent or cross the road, we must pack something that makes dealing with these challenges more manageable. Grace is that combination of love, forgiveness, forbearance, compassion, and tact that comes in handy when circumstances and people frustrate and disappoint us. When drivers cut us off in traffic, waitresses mess up our order, or co-workers forget a crucial meeting, we don't consider them deserving of grace. In more serious situations, it may be necessary to give more grace than we think we can possibly offer. But God calls us to extend grace anyway.

We think of grace principally as a New Testament concept, but God has been extending it to man ever since the Garden of Eden. Let's look at one Old Testament patriarch's challenges and how he handled them—with grace.

PACKING MORE THAN PROVISIONS

If there was one man who knew about packing and unpacking, it was Abram. He and his wife, Sarah, wandered all over the Fertile Crescent, Canaan, and even Egypt. Think hundreds of camels, livestock, and tents as well as silver, gold, food and other provisions, and you have an idea what moving their caravan entailed. This group included Abram's nephew, Lot, whom Abram took into his household when God called Abram to go to Canaan (Genesis 12:5).

Lot came along for the ride, and like Abram, was blessed in the process. In fact, Abram and Lot had so many livestock that their new home in Canaan couldn't provide enough water and pasture for both their herds. Quarreling broke out among their herdsman.

Abram offered a solution to their problem. It appears that he took Lot up to an outlook. Abram offered Lot first choice of the surrounding land, and he would take the rest. For Lot, it was a no-brainer. One look at the fertile, lush plain of Jordan probably reminded him of Egypt, where they had just visited. Lot might have longed for a similar life in the plain. So he chose the plain of Jordan, pitching his tent near Sodom and eventually moving into the city itself.

Abram might have seemed foolish to unselfishly offer this kind of grace to his nephew, but Abram remembered that God had promised him and his descendants all the land he could see. In fact, God told him to "walk through the length and breath of the land" to lay claim to it (Genesis 13:17). In response, Abram built an altar to worship God at Hebron.

In contrast, Lot did not seem to honor his uncle for his gift of grace. Since Abram was older, Lot should have deferred in respect to his uncle when considering his choices. Abram had cared for Lot for years after Lot's father, Haran, died, and Lot should have shown gratitude for that protection. Instead, Lot took what looked like the best while Abram was left with the rest.

Abram trusted that God would take care of him as He had promised. He walked in faith; Lot walked by sight. Lot's opportunism and selfishness eventually led him into more problems, which later drew Abram into more conflict involving his nephew.

FIGHTING FOR LOT

Abram was willing to go to great lengths to protect his nephew Lot—even to become a warrior. When the local kings of five city-states of the Dead Sea (including Sodom, Lot's home) rebelled against four kings from the East, Lot was right in the middle of it. War broke out, and Lot was captured by the coalition from the East, along with his possessions and other captives.

Taking his duty as Lot's protector seriously, Abram led his 318 trained men on a night raid that surprised the enemy, who fled so quickly they left their plunder behind. Abram's army recovered Lot, his goods, and the rest of the captives.

Later God shared His plan to destroy the wicked city of Sodom with Abraham (God had changed his name). Abraham extended grace to Lot again by negotiating with God to save the city for only 10 righteous men from destruction. The next morning, as Abraham looked toward Sodom and Gomorrah at the dense smoke rising from the land, he trusted that God kept His promise and protected Lot (Genesis 18:16-33). Scripture tells us that God listened to Abraham's petition: "So when God destroyed the cities of the plain, he remembered Abraham, and he brought Lot out of the catastrophe that overthrew the cities where Lot had lived" (Genesis 19:29).

God extended grace to Abraham and, in turn, Abraham

extended grace to Lot. God offered land to Abraham, and Abraham offered land to Lot. God rescued Abraham from kings, and Abraham rescued Lot from kings. Abraham messed up, and God still loved him. Lot messed up, too, and Abraham still loved him. We can see how Abraham mirrored God's grace to him by extending grace to Lot.

UNDERSTANDING GRACE

When God offered grace to Abraham, the patriarch understood what it meant to receive grace. By extending grace to Lot, Abraham understood what it took to give grace and he could better appreciate God's mercy and goodness even more. Every time Abraham offered grace to Lot, the patriarch gave a face to the concept of grace.

The same is true for us. Each time we partake of God's grace, we learn more about who God is and who we should be. The more we offer grace to others, even when they don't deserve it, we see how merciful God is to extend it to us as His undeserving children. It is only by giving and receiving God's grace that we can live the abundant lives He offers us. So it is important to understand what grace is and what it isn't.

People in the world have different concepts of grace. Some people think that grace is a blanket tolerance of sin. They reason that no matter what the crime, it's okay with God because He loves everyone, and we are all sinners. Others believe that grace is a display of weakness, an invitation to be a perpetual doormat to be taken advantage by others. Some even think grace means a refusal to confront sin because Jesus commands us not to judge.

Sadly, even some Christians don't grasp the transforming power that grace can have in their daily lives. Some see amazing grace as limited only to their conversion. Others feel compelled to work their way to heaven, chalking up their good deeds like a scorecard. Still others think that grace is a privilege deserved by a chosen few, a group to which they smugly belong.

Grace is none of these mistaken ideas. Jesus was "full of grace and truth" (John 1:14), yet He did not tolerate sin nor was He afraid to confront it (John 8:1-11). He was the most forgiving man on earth, yet He was also the most courageous (Luke 23:32-34). We will never deserve grace no matter how hard we work for God (Ephesians 2:4-9).

The truth is that we have all messed up (Romans 3:22-26). God sent His Son Jesus to die for us even while we were still sinners (Romans 5:6-8). Our sinless Lord took the penalty of our sins on Himself to be sin so we could become righteous (2 Corinthians 5:21). He paid the price to offer us grace (Ephesians 1:3-8). We have the privilege to live a super-abundant life through faith and obedience to God now and in eternity (Romans 6:1-14). God's grace to us shows us what grace really means. For that, we should ever be thankful.

SHOWERS OF GRACE

Grace falls as a continual shower of God's blessings on us. But it should not stop with us. As author Richard Blackaby writes, "We are not called to just bathe in grace; we are to shower it upon others."[1] He writes that instead, some Christians "are like spiritual sponges soaking up grace to the saturation point. Yet you have to put the squeeze on them to get any back out."[2] Instead of sprinkling showers of blessing, they douse others with acid rain.

We need to see others through God's "grace lens" as He sees them–broken but not beyond repair. Just like He "fixes" us daily with our faults and failings, so we can have the same grace with others who are works in progress. None of us have arrived but, with God's help, we are on our way. We should not give up on others. God has not given up on us.

So how can we scatter God's grace? How can we put a face on grace? How does it translate to our world today? Here are some examples:

- Encourage your crabby coworker (Ephesians 4:29).

- Allow someone to go ahead of you in line (Philippians 2:3-4).
- Forgive your Christian sister's thoughtless remark (Ephesians 4:32).
- Apologize for your angry tirade today (Ephesians 5:26).
- Wish the obnoxious customer a good day (Roman 12:17-21).
- Affirm your family members whenever you can (1 Thessalonians 5:11).
- Admit you messed up and go on (Philippians 3:13-14).

You can see that these are simple actions, but they have the potential to change the world—one person at a time. The best place to start is with that person in the mirror. Sometimes it is really difficult to extend grace to ourselves, but we can do it.

EXTENDING GRACE TO OURSELVES
Peter was so sure of himself when he told Christ, "I will never disown you" (Matthew 26:35). After all, as a disciple, he was close to Jesus and would never do such a thing. But he did. Then Peter realized what he had done and wept bitterly. It was hard to extend grace to himself. After His resurrection, the Lord didn't send Peter packing. Instead He offered grace to one whose intentions fell so short.

How often do our expectations run high and then we don't deliver? Sometimes we expect exemplary results from ourselves and when we fail, we become terribly disappointed and discouraged like Peter. We can be hard to live with. We can be hard to live with ourselves.

If we have a hard time offering grace to ourselves, it can help to express our feelings to a trusted friend, minister, or counselor. Journaling can also serve as a way to express our thoughts in writing. It is more helpful to write about what we have learned from the experience rather than just reliving the emotions surrounding the event over and over. This can help us move on with our lives.[3] King David "journaled" his feelings in the Psalms, especially Psalm 51, when he found it difficult to forgive himself after committing adultery and murder in his affair with Bathsheba.

When we fail, we can choose to view our mistakes as opportunities for growth and learn from them. In some instances, we may even one day be able to laugh at them. When we learn to accept our failings, we can trust that God will forgive. We can even learn to offer grace to ourselves.

IS IT IMPOSSIBLE?

Some people may say that in certain situations, extending grace is just impossible. But one woman would disagree. She experienced the devastating loss of her son and still found it possible to forgive.

Scarlett Lewis learned in Bible school that Jesus taught us to forgive, and she has tried to forgive others. But her resolve was put to the test at Sandy Hook Elementary when a disturbed young man murdered six teachers and administrators along with 20 first graders, her son, Jesse, among them.

As time went on, Scarlett knew she should try to overcome her hatred and anger for her son's killer and extend grace to him. She discovered he felt isolated, had emotional issues, and was estranged from his father. This in no way excused his actions but it helped her better understand why he did what he did. She also found that she needed to extend grace to herself for not being a "perfect mother" so she could focus on the present and be a better mother to her older son. She learned to consciously replace regrets with good memories and this has helped her in the healing process.

There are days when she still feels vengeful. She then realizes that similar feelings caused her son's killer's rampage. At those times, she makes a conscious choice to forgive—again.

She finds that she can forgive only with God's help. Even when the circumstances seem too difficult or painful to forgive,

God helped her do the impossible. She writes, "On days when I'm feeling low and angry, I look skyward and exclaim, 'God, I guess you think I am strong enough to handle this.' Then I step back and remember that forgiveness is for me—for my life and for the lives of those around me—and I forgive once again." [4]

Forgiveness is for all of us. If we are faithful, God keeps on forgiving us—again and again and again. His grace is indescribable. When we pack grace, how can we keep it just for ourselves?

ARE WE THERE YET?

1. What was Abram's solution to the quarrel between Abram's and Lot's herdsman? What lasting consequences did Lot's choice have (2 Peter 2:7-8)?

2. How was God's grace for Abraham mirrored in the patriarch's grace for Lot?

3. What are some examples of God's dealings with man in the Bible that demonstrate His gracious nature?

4. Who else in the Bible extended grace to people when they didn't deserve it?

5. Who demonstrates to us the supreme meaning of grace? Why?

6. What are some simple ways to scatter God's grace in our everyday lives?

7. What are some qualities of grace in action (1 Corinthians 13:4-7)?

8. What are some misconceptions people have about grace?

9. Why is it sometimes difficult to offer grace to ourselves? What are some ways to help us move beyond this?

10. What are some ways we can encourage our family and friends when they offer grace in their encounters with others?

TRIP TIPS: Remembering Not to Forget

Whether our forgetfulness is born of age, anxiety, or just plain absent-mindedness, we all have forgotten something. When this happens, we sometimes beat ourselves up, especially when we let other people down. We need to allow ourselves grace, let it go, and try to do better next time.

God knows our tendency to forget and often told His people to remember. Whether it was smearing blood on a doorpost, piling up stones, or celebrating a special meal, He gave them tangible memorials so they would not forget.

Today with our lives so fragmented, it can be difficult to remember everything. Here are some ideas to help lighten your memory load.

Tickler files (3 x 5 cards or larger labeled 1-31) can remind you to do certain tasks like paying your bills monthly. Or you can set the alarm on your phone or computer. Carry sticky notes in case you want to post your reminders.

Triggers also jog our memories. Some triggers involve *time* like scheduling your Bible study time daily *after breakfast* or filling up the car with gas *every Tuesday after work* so you won't forget. Other triggers involve *place* like praying for the sick *after passing the hospital* or putting your keys *near your purse and phone*, ready to head out the door.

Regular routines also help you remember. To remember to take your vitamins and/or medicine, store your medicine bottle or pillbox *near the table if you take them with meals* (just keep them out of reach of children). For another visual cue, *check off a chart* with medicines and times they should be taken daily. It's the little changes that can make a big difference to help you remember.

BAGGAGE CLAIM

"Life is an adventure in forgiveness." Norman Cousins

"When you forgive, you in no way change the past—but you sure do change the future." Bernard Meltzer

"Do your little bit of good where you are; it's those little bits of good put together that overwhelm the world." Desmond Tutu

"For grace is given not because we have done good works, but in order that we may be able to do them." Saint Augustine of Hippo

"Our worst days are never so bad that you are beyond the reach of God's grace. And your best days are never so good that you are beyond the need of God's grace." Jerry Bridges

"Always forgive your enemies—nothing annoys them so much." Oscar Wilde

BRING IT ON HOME

What one thing can you do this week to lighten your load by packing more grace into your life? Write it here:

CHAPTER 4

PATIENCE
Learning to Carry Some Wait

"Hope is patience with the lamp lit."

Tertullian

Air travel might be the fastest transportation available, but it certainly requires a lot of waiting. We hurry up to wait. We wait to check in, wait to pass security check, wait to board, and wait to find our seat. Depending on the weather and time of year, it can be enough to test our patience to its limit. So it's wise to pack something to amuse ourselves. Otherwise, we'll be spending a lot a time people watching—and waiting.

In the same way, life moves along at break-neck speed, but paradoxically, we spend a lot of time waiting. We can't wait to grow up, graduate, find a job, get married, buy a home, have kids, and retire, but there's a lot of waiting in the meantime. We wait for so many things, yet something else to try our patience is just around the corner. As author Henry Miller once observed, "Life, as it is called, is for most of us one long postponement."

So how do we face life's endless waiting? Do we blow up in exasperation, seethe in prickly frustration, or face it patiently— one minute at a time? It took years for one young man's dreams to come true. Yet he found the patience to face his trials with the Lord's help.

THE DREAMER'S NIGHTMARE
Seventeen year-old Joseph had amazing dreams, but one day his

life morphed into a nightmare. His ten older brothers gave new meaning to the term *sibling rivalry*. They didn't just hate or envy him. They wanted him dead (Genesis 37). They didn't appreciate how Joseph took their father, Jacob, a bad report about four of them tending their flocks. His dreams of them all bowing down to him didn't help their relationship either.

To make matters worse, Jacob loved Joseph more than any of them because he was born to his beloved wife, Rachel. To demonstrate his preferential affection, Jacob gave Joseph a richly ornamented robe, possibly with long sleeves, which made manual labor difficult. Not only did this beautiful coat of many colors show Jacob's partiality to his favored son, but it could also excuse Joseph from some of the work. No wonder Joseph's brothers could not speak a kind word to him.

This family conflict reached a breaking point when Jacob sent Joseph to check on his brothers tending the sheep away from home. When they saw him coming, they immediately plotted to kill him. To prevent bloodshed, Reuben persuaded them to put Joseph in a dry cistern so he could later rescue him. While Reuben was gone, Midianite traders came riding by and gave Judah an idea. Why not sell Joseph as a slave to the merchants and pick up some silver in the bargain? Amid Joseph's cries of protest, his brothers sold him for 20 pieces of silver and rid themselves of the "dreamer" forever...or so they thought. They took Joseph's coat, which they had dipped in goat's blood, back to their father who imagined the worst and grieved for his dead son torn apart by a wild animal.

THE PATH TO PATIENCE

As Joseph struggled as a slave on the long journey from Dothan to Egypt, his situation seemed hopeless. But he had a choice. He could grow bitter and angry about his plight or he could trust in the God of his father, Jacob.

Jacob was about 91 years old by the time Joseph was born

and no doubt was an older, wiser father.[1] To his credit, he and his wife Rachel had instilled in Joseph qualities in which his older brothers did not excel. Joseph knew about God. He knew about faithfulness, purity, and forgiveness. He also knew how God had blessed his parents with his birth and the birth of his brother, Benjamin, after so many years of waiting. So Joseph was no stranger to patience. His life as a slave and prisoner in Egypt developed this trait further and paved his path to patience in several ways.

Patience with People ~ Joseph's father's preferential treatment fanned the flame of hate and resentment from his brothers and culminated in their selling him into Egyptian slavery. Though Joseph served Potiphar faithfully, Potiphar's wife accused him falsely and Potiphar banished him to prison. Though he interpreted Pharaoh's cupbearer's dream correctly, Joseph was forgotten in prison. While he waited, he forgave (Genesis 39-40).

Patience with Circumstances ~ The circumstances of Joseph's life were less than ideal. His dysfunctional family was rife with favoritism, deceit, and hatred. Although he tried to live right, it seemed things went terribly wrong. We know he unjustly spent at least two years in prison, but it could have been more. Joseph's treatment there was described in Psalm 105:18: "They bruised his feet with shackles, his neck was put in irons." These circumstances were beyond his control. While he waited, he was faithful.

Patience with God's Will ~ During his 13 years of slavery and imprisonment, Joseph must have felt isolated, lonely, and misunderstood. He could have rebelled against God in frustration and resentment. He could have given in to the daily temptation of Potiphar's wife, taken personal credit for interpreting Pharaoh's dreams, and retaliated against his brothers for treating him so cruelly. Instead he honored God and His will in each circumstance. He refused the sexual advances of Potiphar's wife, gave God the glory for the interpretation of Pharaoh's dreams, and freely forgave his brothers. He acknowledged God's hand in what happened in his life and realized that it was all for good in spite of the circumstances (Genesis 45:7-8; 50:20-21; Romans 8:28). While he waited, he trusted in God.

In time God blessed Joseph by making him a ruler second only to Pharaoh. His administrative experience in Potiphar's house prepared him for his role in providing food for many during the seven years of famine. In the process the Lord worked His will in providing a new home in Egypt for Jacob, his family, and eventually their descendants in a fertile, peaceful land where they could grow and multiply into a great nation. Through all this, Joseph developed patience in circumstances that he would not have chosen, but he endured because he waited on God's timing.

STUCK IN A HOLDING PATTERN

Waiting on God's timing can feel like being stuck in a holding pattern. One of the most frustrating times on a plane trip can be when we are several thousand feet in the air, circling the runway below. We are so ready to get where we are going. Instead we are flying around and around, waiting for clearance to land.

In life we can be stuck in a holding pattern, too. We are waiting for something, but for some reason we can't move on to get it. We are waiting for the right man to come along. Or we are waiting for the adoption to be finalized. Or we are waiting for the perfect job, the debt to be paid, the addiction to be overcome. It's like the children of Israel felt in the wilderness. They wanted to move on with their lives and settle in the Promised Land, the land that flowed with milk and honey. Instead they were stuck in the desert with water and quail (and they were sick of that). They just seemed to be circling around Mount Sinai.

But in the process, God fed them, nurtured them, and protected them, and they got to know Him better. Note how God described His tender care during their wanderings: "Then I said to you, 'Do not be in dread or afraid of them. The LORD your God, who goes before you, will himself fight for you, just as he did for you in Egypt before your eyes, and in the wilderness, where you have seen how the LORD your God carried you, as a man carries his son, all the way that you went until you came to this place'" (Deuteronomy 1:29-31).

When the children of Israel were in a holding pattern, God held them in His arms. He will hold us, too. If we let God nurture us when we are stuck in life's holding patterns, we can know Him in a more personal way than we have ever known Him before. Relationships take time, and sometimes it takes longer than we think it should. It is that time of waiting that helps us build our trust in Him to richer, deeper levels. He wants to prepare us for what is coming next. We don't know the future, but He does and He wants us to be ready. [2]

A "JUST CAN'T WAIT" CULTURE

We need to be ready because we will face people and situations that will try our patience daily. In our busy lives, it is difficult for us to wait. We grow impatient with the sales clerk who charges us too much, the child who can't understand the math problem, and the new neighbor who can't speak English. We switch lanes several times at the store to find the fastest checkout. We move heavy boxes ourselves because we are too impatient to wait for help. We abandon an online video if it takes more than five seconds to load.

Our world of instant gratification and hyperconnectivity through the latest device makes patience a rare commodity. With terms in our current vocabulary like *fast track, rat race,* and *quick fix,* the whole concept of patience is counter-culture. For the Christian, patience can carry a deeper meaning than just waiting. In the Bible, it can imply persevering and standing strong through hardship or trying circumstances. Not everyone is willing to do that in a culture that just can't wait.

When we pack our bags with patience, we are contrary to culture. So how do we develop patience while we go against the flow of the world?

Identify your triggers. Sometimes specific things just push your buttons. Think about what causes you to lose your patience and ask yourself, "Why?" Sometimes physical factors can affect your patience like fatigue, hunger, and dehydration. Maybe it is a certain situation, person, or phrase. Ask your family and friends for insights. Knowing your triggers can help you either to avoid them or prepare for them. For example, if a talkative co-worker drives you crazy while you are trying to work, politely excuse yourself before you grow impatient.

Slow down. Slowing down and acting patient can help you feel more patient. By eating your food more slowly, you can learn to enjoy your food, eat less, and train yourself to be less impulsive in other areas. By breathing in slowly through your nose and out through your mouth several times, you can relax your body, slow your heart rate, and distance yourself from a stressful situation. This can help you lighten your stress load. James wrote, "Know this, my beloved brothers; let every person be quick to hear, slow to speak, slow to anger" (James 1:19).

Realize that impatience doesn't help. How many honking horns will alleviate a traffic jam? The truth is that impatience rarely speeds things along. Instead it can clutter your mind and misdirect your energy to deal with your situation. It is much better to acknowledge that sometimes you can't change what happens, so you will just have to wait, "with all humility and gentleness, with patience, bearing with one another in love" (Ephesians 4:2).

Try to understand. It is easier to grow impatient with someone you don't understand or know. Even if you think you understand someone's motives, you might not know the whole story. It can help to ask questions to clarify your understanding and then really listen to get a fuller perspective. "He who answers before listening—that is his folly and his shame" (Proverbs 18:13).

Let it go. Everyone occasionally has a bad day, and it sometimes shows. Perhaps your boss had a family crisis. Your friend might be sick and short-tempered. Maybe your neighbor lost his job and is hypercritical. Resolve to let it go. Don't keep a record of wrongs (1 Corinthians 13:4-5). "Good sense makes one slow to anger, and it is his glory to overlook an offense" (Proverbs 19:11).

Know what patience isn't. Being patient doesn't mean that we must remain in an unhealthy friendship, immoral liaison, or dangerous situation just because we are commanded to be patient with the way things are. Nor does it mean to tolerate or condone sin in the hopes that one day it might get better if we are patient enough. In teaching others, Paul exhorted Timothy to "reprove, rebuke, and exhort, with complete patience and teaching" but also to "always be soberminded" (2 Timothy 4:2, 5). Paul was advocating common sense. Sometimes it is best not to wait but to flee like Joseph did on one occasion.

Be patient with yourself. When you want so much to be in control but are not, it helps to practice self-compassion. Sometimes you have to tell yourself, "I'm not perfect but that's okay. I'll do my best right now." Francis de Sales echoed this sentiment: "Have patience with all things, but chiefly have patience with yourself. Do not lose courage in considering your own imperfections, but instantly set about remedying them—every day begin the task anew."

Remember how God is patient with you. When you start to yell at the kids for tracking in mud on your clean floor, it will help to think how many times God has been patient with you. The psalmist said it well: "The LORD is merciful and gracious, slow to anger and abounding in steadfast love. He does not always chide, nor will he keep his anger forever. He does not deal with us according to our sins, nor repay us according to our iniquities" (Psalm 103:8-10).

LIFE'S WAITING ROOM

Life has been likened to a waiting room. We are always waiting for something. Sometimes we can leave the waiting room fairly quickly, like Peter's friends did when he miraculously escaped prison in answer to their prayers. Other times it takes months, even years, like the birth of Hannah's long-awaited son Samuel. Sometimes we may never get things we are waiting for, like Paul's answer from God regarding the removal of his thorn of the flesh. But sometimes we receive something in life's waiting room that is better than we could ever imagine, like Joseph's reunion with his estranged family and his rise from prison to palace.

Life is filled with uncertainty, but some things are certain: God knows best, He is in control, and He will be with us while we wait. As Isaiah proclaimed, "From of old no one has heard or perceived by ear, no eye has seen a God besides you, who acts for those who wait for him" (Isaiah 64:4).

ARE WE THERE YET?

1. What part did Jacob's favoritism play in Joseph's brothers' hatred of their younger brother? How did Joseph's dreams make it worse?

2. What was the significance of coats in the life of Joseph?

3. How did embracing God's will help Joseph develop patience with the people and circumstances in his life? How did he exemplify Isaiah 40:30-31?

4. How does Psalm 105:18 give us insight into the way prisoners were commonly treated during Joseph's lifetime? How did Joseph's time in prison prepare him for his later role in Pharaoh's service?

5. Who were some patient Bible characters? Who were some impatient Bible characters?

6. Why is patience in our world today so counter culture?

7. Why is it helpful to identify triggers that can test our patience?

8. What are some ways slowing down can help us be more patient?

9. Why is it potentially dangerous to remain in some situations because we are waiting for things to get better?

10. What are some ways to help us develop more patience? What certainties about God can help us while we wait?

TRIP TIPS: Writing While You Wait

In the airline terminal or doctor's office, why grow impatient waiting or playing that game on your smartphone *again*? Instead take a few minutes that can make a world of difference to someone. Pack some cards for writing short notes when you travel or wait for appointments. To save time and money, keep several on hand to be prepared to send them for any occasion.

Receiving snail mail is a rare treat these days, so handwritten cards are especially appreciated. Personal written notes can be priceless and treasured for a long time by the recipient. It's a thoughtful way to show you care to anyone who is sick, shut-in, discouraged, or away from home (Colossians 3:12).

Your message doesn't have to be long, fancy, or profound— just speak from your heart. If you have trouble finding the right words, check out Jane McWhorter's book *Special Delivery: A Course in Letter-Writing.*[3] The author gives examples of what to say in a variety of circumstances and these can give you ideas of how to put your thoughts on paper. Often including a Scripture, quotation, or pithy saying can lift someone's spirits.

Sending e-cards from your laptop or smartphone is another way to let others know you remember them. Some e-cards are free on the Internet and take just a few minutes to fill out. The more sophisticated ones have fees but the professional animation with music can make it worth it. On an appropriate occasion, who wouldn't be delighted to receive a card with the character(s) singing the message!

BAGGAGE CLAIM

"Patience is something you admire in the driver behind you and scorn in the one ahead." Mac McCleary

"If you are patient in one moment of anger, you will escape a hundred days of sorrow." Chinese Proverb

"The secret of patience is to do something in the meantime." Unknown

"Patience with others is love. Patience with self is hope. Patience with God is faith." Adel Bestavros

"Just because something isn't happening for you right now doesn't mean that it will never happen." Unknown

"You can learn many things from children—how much patience you have, for instance." Franklin P. Jones

BRING IT ON HOME

What one thing can you do this week to lighten your load by packing more patience into your life? Write it here:

_____

CHAPTER 5

RESOURCEFULNESS
Giving Back What You Have Been Given

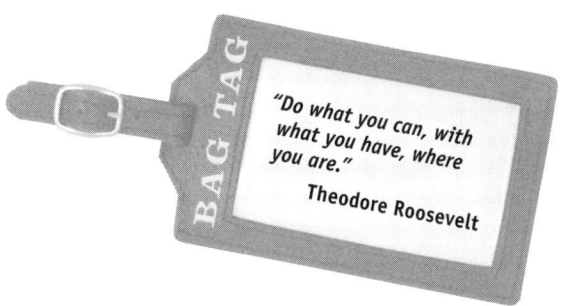

"Do what you can, with what you have, where you are."

Theodore Roosevelt

S ometimes travelers have had to be really resourceful when they pack for a trip. For example, in the days before GPS, they actually had to know where they were going. If they were directionally challenged, they would pack a map, a large piece of paper that was extremely difficult to fold back flat to its original shape. Folding the map was really a test of the traveler's skill. The mapmakers figured if travelers couldn't fold the map back like it was, they probably would have a hard time finding their destination. If the travelers got lost, they usually sent a male to ask for directions, which often proved to be more difficult than finding the right road!

In the book of Exodus, if the children of Israel got lost in their flight from Egypt, they probably did not have a map, and there would be few populated places in the wilderness to stop and ask for directions. However, they were blessed with their own GPS (God's Providential Steering), which led them with a cloud by day and a pillar of fire by night. God didn't take the shortest route to the Promised Land, but instead led them to wander for 40 years. It was during this period that God gave Moses the Law, including the instructions for building the tabernacle. Just how resourceful were these desert pilgrims in furnishing it?

WILDERNESS WILLINGNESS

Escape from Egyptian slavery gave the Israelites a new life of freedom, but it wasn't long before they were grumbling, quarrelling, and even revolting against their leader, Moses. They convinced Moses' brother, Aaron, to fashion a golden calf, which they worshiped for bringing them out of Egypt. Their rebellion and lack of faith prompted the Lord to delay their journey until all the unfaithful over 20 years of age perished in the desert.

However, there was a time when it seemed the people were united in one purpose. On Mt. Sinai for 40 days and nights, Moses had been rewriting God's Law on stone tablets. Within these laws, the Lord gave them an opportunity to build and furnish a dwelling place for God on earth, the tabernacle. The Lord commanded:

> *From what you have,* take an offering for the LORD. Everyone who is willing is to bring to the LORD an offering of gold, silver and bronze; blue, purple and scarlet yarn and fine linen; goat hair; ram skins dyed red and another type of durable leather; acacia wood; olive oil for the light; spices for the anointing oil and for the fragrant incense; and onyx stones and other gems to be mounted on the ephod and breastpiece (Exodus 35:5-9) (Italics the author's).

Such a call for willing hearts and hands brought out the best in the people's resourcefulness. Suddenly they had a purpose in their on-the-move existence, and they gave their time to the work at hand. Soon the camp was buzzing with men and women designing, crafting, weaving, spinning, cutting, setting, mounting, and woodworking. With skill and ingenuity, they created beautiful clothing for the priests and fine furnishings for the Tabernacle. God blessed the two craftsmen, Bezalel and Oholiab, with special talent and handpicked them to lead in teaching others the how-to process.

The people also found resources from their own treasures—

precious stones, gold, silver, bronze, skins, hides, spices, olive oil, colorful yarns, and fine linen. Shopping for such a variety of supplies at their local discount store in the desert was not possible so where did these come from? They did not leave empty-handed when they fled Egypt. God told the Israelites to ask the Egyptians for what they wanted (Exodus 12:33-36). In fact, they "plundered" the Egyptians. So when Moses requested provisions for the tabernacle, God's people freely gave of what they had. Soon Moses had to ask them to stop because there was more than enough (Exodus 36:6-7). This is one time when God's people were so resourceful that they were giving too much.

Finally when the work was finished, Moses inspected everything and blessed the people because they had followed the Lord's instructions. The tabernacle was a sanctuary for God's visual presence. Now the people could look at the cloud over the tabernacle by day or fire in the cloud by night and know that the glory of the Lord was with them (Exodus 39:43; 40:34-38). They gave of their resources and, in turn, were blessed.

WASTE NOT, WANT NOT

Closer to home, another example of resourcefulness for a noble cause was the American effort on the home front during World War II. Because so many everyday commodities were needed for the war effort, citizens were asked to do their part to "use it up, make it do, wear it out" to stretch their resources. Necessities were rationed and "doing without" was the norm. President Franklin D. Roosevelt called on Americans to contribute scrap rubber like old raincoats, bathing caps, garden hoses, and rubber shoes to make new tires. They brought in waste kitchen fats to make explosives and collected scrap brass and copper for artillery shells. Even children harvested milkweed for lifejackets! With the country working together, there was a sense of generosity and unity toward a common goal. [1, 2]

Fast-forward to today in America, and it's a different story.

Instead of resourcefulness, our country is known as a "throw-away society." According to EPA 2013 statistics, individual Americans generate 4.40 pounds of garbage daily.[3] This includes food we throw away, broken products we can't or won't fix, and objects we abandon for newer counterparts. From clothes to cameras to furniture, ours is a disposable society. As wit Andy Rooney put it, "Americans put their whole lives by the side of the road to be carted away Monday, Wednesday, and Friday...Recycling is an unsubstantiated rumor."

Fortunately, this is changing. We are realizing how precious our resources are and how we cannot continue to waste them. As Christians we understand that the earth is the Lord's, but He has entrusted us with its care (Psalm 8:3-8). Mankind's ignorance, carelessness, and greed have robbed the earth of many of its natural resources. As God's people, we should be examples in good stewardship. There is a balance between the extremes of worshiping "Mother Earth" and ignoring or neglecting our responsibility because "it's going to burn up anyway!" We can each start by making small changes in our daily lives and when all these efforts are put together, they can make a big difference.

RENEWING OUR MINDS AND RESOURCES

Of all the renewable resources we have, the most important is our minds. Paul reminds us to be "transformed by the renewing of our minds" (Romans 12:2). We are to be constantly open to how we can please God, not the world, and use the gifts He has given us to serve others (1 Peter 4:10-11).

Jesus' simple but encompassing statement "that nothing may be lost" is still true today (John 6:12). How can we wisely use all our resources to be sure nothing is wasted? There are so many ways to utilize what God has already provided. You might already be doing some or all of these things. Challenge yourself to see what else you can do with what you have.

For example, we extend our nonrenewable reserves of oil by

planning our routes to take fewer trips and walking or biking when we can. By using both sides of our paper, we can save forests. By growing our own food, choosing smaller portions at buffets, and eating all we choose, we can stretch our food supply and avoid waste. By taking shorter showers and using a rain barrel to save water for our yards and gardens, we save clean water for where it is critically needed. By taking care of our physical and mental health and valuing our time, we also show respect for two other nonrenewable resources, our bodies and our time.[3]

REDUCE, RECYCLE AND REUSE—THEN AND NOW

Think about it—thousands of years ago when the Israelites generously gave their gifts for the tabernacle, they were utilizing the "Reduce, Recycle, Reuse" motto of today. Here are a few simple reminders to help us do the same.

Use lawn clippings to mulch your shrubs. Plan a "grab, root, and growl" night for leftovers each week. Purchase products with less packaging. When practical, buy reusable products, like beverage containers, gift bags, and shopping bags. Maintain your car and appliances so they will last longer. Learn simple home repairs.

Find out what local recycling is available. Check the EPA website for ways to recycle eyeglasses, paper, glass, plastic, and aluminum. Certain stores and manufacturers offer options for donating or recycling toner cartridges, computers, cell phones, and TVs. Be sure to note the special disposal procedures for products like batteries, oils, paints, pesticides, and used tires.[4]

The children of Israel were blessed for sharing their resources. What about us? Will we be like the two servants in Jesus' parable of the talents who did what they could with what they were given? Or will we be like the one-talent servant who hid his talent? He misused what the master entrusted to him and acted irresponsibly. Instead of multiplying the possibilities, he buried what he was given and received the master's condemnation (Matthew 25:24-30). The point of the parable was not how much each of the servants was given, but what they chose to do with the resources at their disposal. Let's pray for wisdom to use the resources God has given each of us in the best way that we can.

GENEROSITY IS THE KEY

For all their shortcomings in their wilderness, when the Israelites' gave of themselves and their resources, they got it right. Generosity is the key to their resourcefulness and the key to ours. When we are resourceful, it gives us the means to share with others. No passage exemplifies this overflowing attitude better than 2 Corinthians 9:6-8: "The point is this: whoever sows sparingly will also reap sparingly, and whoever sows bountifully will also reap bountifully. Each one must give as he has decided in his heart, not reluctantly or under complusion, for God loves a cheerful giver. And God is able to make all grace abound to you, so that having all sufficiency in all things at all times, you may abound in every good work."

Paul continued that our generosity not only benefits others but ourselves as well. We will be made rich in every way so we can continue to give, which ultimately results in thanksgiving to God. Resourcefulness stretches the resources we have so that more may benefit. When we lighten our loads by sharing our resources, we make the most of what God has given us. We are so blessed that we often take what we have for granted. We forget that many people go to bed hungry each night not only in Third World countries but also in our own.

SHARING WHAT WE HAVE

There are many ways we can share our resources with others. Healing Hands International (HHI) is an amazing example of what Christians joining together can do in our country and abroad. HHI participates in disaster relief, provides medical supplies, and drills wells to provide clean water. They teach food sustainability, including drip irrigation, fish farming, and small animal husbandry to those who need it to live. They also have organized "Women Worth a Million," a program that trains women in underdeveloped countries to use their talents to make shea butter, jewelry, and apparel. The sale of these products provides income for these women and their families and gives them a sense of dignity and worth in their own God-given abilities. When we serve others by supporting such organizations, we serve Christ (Matthew 25:40).

There are other efforts locally and nationally to share knowledge and resources. Check out how you can use your time and talents to stretch resources like community gardens, food collections, home building projects, clothing giveaways, homeless meals/ sunshine bags, disaster/crisis aid, and student tutoring. Consider getting involved in World English Institute (online) or Let's Start Talking (face-to-face), two efforts in the church using the Bible to teach English. The Lord only knows how many people can be touched with the gospel through these efforts.

We don't have to be a part of an organized effort to use our skills and resources to care about others. God can use our gifts in personal ways. A friend found a great deal of satisfaction cleaning houses of members who were dealing with grief or supporting family members in long-term care. She considered her gift something small, but her contribution was priceless to the recipient.

Just like the children of Israel must have marveled at the beauty of the colors, textures, and handwork of the tabernacle and its furnishings, so we are amazed at what can be done when we put our resources together. With God, the possibilities are endless.

ARE WE THERE YET?

1. What does it mean to be resourceful? What are some resources that God has given us?

2. What were the materials for the tabernacle that God requested from the Israelites? How did the Lord provide them?

3. What were some ways that Americans on the home front during World War II were called to be resourceful? What are some parallels with the children of Israel providing for the tabernacle?

4. How did these Bible characters use items at hand to accomplish.God's work? Moses (Exodus 7:10), Gideon (Judges 7:17-18), Elisha (2 Kings 2:19-22).

5. How did these Bible characters waste the resources God provided for them? Prodigal Son (Luke 15:11-32), Foolish servant (Matthew 25:14-30).

6. Why should Christians be good examples in the wise use of resources?

7. How was the principle of respect for God's creation in plants and animals demonstrated in Deuteronomy 20:19-20; 22:6-7? How can we show this kind of respect today?

8. Why has the U.S. been labeled "The Disposable Society"? What are some ways we can reverse this "disposable" trend to make our God-given resources go further?

9. What are some ways we can "reduce, reuse, and recycle" in our local communities?

10. How can stretching our own resources enable us to be generous to others?

TRIP TIPS: Fashion that's Fun and Frugal

Women in ancient times might have shopped 'til they dropped, but there is no doubt that they loved fine clothes and accessories (1 Peter 3:3). Fine things were expensive back then as they are now. These days paying full price for clothes in the mall can make a big dent in your budget so is there an alternative?

Today a less costly choice is resale shopping. Find a clean, organized store with reasonable prices, and you'll see why this is so popular. In larger stores you will discover a varied inventory of many types of clothes, including some gently used name brands. Sometimes you will find new clothes, with their original tags, donated from stores to make room for new inventory.

There are humanitarian and eco-advantages as well. By buying and donating items to charitable organizations, you support their work. When you recycle your used clothes, it keeps them from ending up in landfills.

However, be aware of the downside of resale shopping. Since clothes are cheaper, it's easy to buy items you don't need or you have something similar. Just because of the price, the "this will do" phenomenon might make you willing to settle for a size that doesn't fit well or a style that "isn't you." If you or a friend can sew, sometimes a small alteration can fix a problem, but this will be inconvenient if you want your purchase ready-to-wear.

Even with these disadvantages, paying a fraction of the retail price for something you love can make up for the disadvantages. If you use shopping savvy and common sense, resale bargain hunting can quickly become one of your favorite sports.

BAGGAGE CLAIM

"If necessity is the mother of invention, then resourcefulness is the father." Beulah Louise Henry

"Act as if what you do makes a difference. It does." William James

"How wonderful it is that nobody need wait a single moment before starting to improve the world." Anne Frank

"We make a living by what we get, but we make a life by what we give." Winston Churchill

"We must live more simply so that others may simply live." Ronald Sider

"Have nothing in your homes that you do not know to be useful and believe to be beautiful." William Morrison

"What you take for granted, others might be praying for." Unknown

BRING IT ON HOME

What one thing can you do this week to lighten your load by packing more resourcefulness into your life? Write it here:

_____

CHAPTER 6

REST
Taking a Break So You Won't Fall Apart

"There's a heavy penalty for resisting a rest."
Phil Callaway

It is ironic that many people who go on vacation get more rest when they return home. After all, they want to get their money's worth for their time "off." They overschedule an hour-by-hour itinerary crammed packed with activities. They overplay so they won't miss a minute of fun. They overpace themselves and are more interested in the distance they cover each day than what they experience. They return home frazzled, cranky, and ready for a vacation!

Our lives can be just like that—packing in too much and covering the distance without enjoying the trip along the way. Soon we realize that we are reaching a breaking point of burnout and exhaustion. We have to do something differently, but what?

A leader in the Old Testament was heading for a similar crisis. He was growing weary by trying to do too much by himself. A wise man gave him some valuable advice, which we can learn from as well.

THE FIRST EFFICIENCY EXPERT IN THE BIBLE

For many people, one of the best things about the end of a hard day's work is going home to their family. Few men knew this better than the Israelite leader, Moses. Probably to protect his family from Pharaoh, Moses had earlier sent away his wife, Zipporah, and their two sons, Gershom and Eliezer, to her father, Jethro, in Midian (Exodus 18:2-4). Now they all were returning to the Israelite camp at Mt. Sinai, and no doubt, Moses was eager to see them. When they arrived, Jethro was delighted to hear how God had rescued the Israelites from the Egyptians, and he honored the Lord with sacrifices (Exodus 18:9-12).

The next day Jethro "went to work" with Moses and observed how he spent his workday. This "efficiency expert" was astounded that Moses was trying to do it all: interpret God's will and then judge how it should be carried out. From morning until evening Moses heard every dispute from any Israelite who needed judgment. It was as if he was serving as a Supreme Court justice on every matter, whether great or small. Jethro counseled Moses, "What you are doing is not good. You and the people with you will certainly wear yourselves out, for the thing is too heavy for you" (Exodus 18:17). Because of the overwhelming workload, the Israelites were not getting justice in a timely manner, and Moses was bone-weary and dog-tired.

To relieve both Moses and the people, Jethro advised Moses to select honest, capable leaders to serve over groups of tens, fifties, hundreds and thousands. These officials would judge the simple cases of the people. Then Moses could serve as teacher and interpreter and be the final judge on the more difficult cases. Moses followed Jethro's suggestion and from then on he had more time to commune with God—and enjoy his family.

REST IS GOD-ORDAINED

Moses learned something important—God's people need to rest. God thought rest was so important that He rested after six days of creation (Genesis 2:1-3). God didn't need a day off—He never sleeps (Psalm 121:3-4). Rather He ceased from His creative labors. He blessed that seventh day and made it holy. By sanctifying the seventh day, He certified that His creation was perfect and complete.

Later God would commemorate the Israelites' deliverance from Egyptian bondage on the seventh day in the Sabbath (Exodus 20: 8-11; Deuteronomy 5:12-15). So on the Sabbath, God's people worshiped the Lord of the exodus and creation. God was so serious about its observance that He decreed that any Israelite found working on that day would be put to death (Exodus 31:15).

He also created the Sabbath to provide man with physical rest. Along with the Israelites, animals, servants, and even foreigners were to take advantage of the rest that the Sabbath provided to be "refreshed" (Exodus 23:12). Later Jesus, as Lord of the Sabbath, emphasized that Sabbath was made for man and not man for the Sabbath (Mark 2:27). Rest is God-ordained. It is good for us, and we need it. Somehow, however, our society has not gotten the message.

RUSHED AND FRAZZLED AND DRAINED—WHO ME?

Though Moses lived thousands of years ago, his problem is as contemporary as jangled nerves, bloodshot eyes, and lack of sleep. Today our society applauds busyness and considers rest frivolous, even lazy. Running in so many directions to get it all done gives many people a kind of rush. Busyness is considered a new kind of high. To them, the busier you are, the more competent, successful, and envied you will seem.[1]

Many women develop a keep-up-or-else mentality to get ahead, but in the end, their methods backfire. To pay for their insatiable wants, some find themselves in an endless cycle of "work and spend," but they are too exhausted and busy working to enjoy their families and what they have. Other women climbing the corporate ladder put in grueling hours only to find that their work suffers from their fatigue and lack of focus. Still others feel so tethered by the demands of their hectic life that they feel like they will never catch up, but they certainly can't stop. No wonder these women feel guilty when they relax.

When women live in overdrive, high gear becomes their

normal speed. Lulls in activity become uncomfortable and abnormal, making it hard to unwind. Just thinking about resting makes them feel restless. When they are "on" all the time, they can't find the "off" switch and eventually they lose the ability to rest at all. Their bodies stay in a fight-or-flight stress response and never return to a calm state. This kind of stress can lead to anxiety, depression, heart disease as well as alcohol, drug or food abuse, which only lead to more problems.

THE AGE OF OVERWORK

As Christian women, we can easily get caught up in this Age of Overwork. After all, doesn't the Bible condemn laziness (Proverbs 10:4; 19:15; Ecclesiastes 10:18)? With the devil so active, how can we sit still (I Peter 5:8)? Aren't we supposed to get all our work done and then rest (John 9:4)? If we examine the context of these passages, they admonish us to work hard and be alert to avoid poverty or disaster. They don't mean that we can never rest. We sometimes have mistaken rest for laziness, but they are not the same.

Whether we work inside or outside the home, the vision of the efficient Proverbs 31 superwoman dances in our heads. After all, she gets up early in the morning and stays up late at night while providing clothes and linens for her household, speaking words of wisdom, and helping the poor. She does all this while running a business on the side and being praised by her family. We feel so *inadequate*. A closer look at the text helps us realize that this lady is an idealized version of the Worthy Woman. It would be difficult for any of us to do all she did.

Let's face it—no matter how hard we try, we will never get all our work done. If we keep trying to fill unreasonable expectations, we will become worn out and burnt out. With all our responsibilities to our God, family, church and community, taking care of ourselves is often the last priority on our to-do list. Sometimes we don't discover how negligent we have been until we are forced to rest because our bodies tell us, "No more!"

When Jesus came to earth, He had to rest. Once He slept so soundly that a furious squall on the Sea of Galilee didn't wake Him (Mark 4:37-38). On two other occasions, Jesus was so busy that He didn't have time to eat (Mark 3:20; 6:30-31). He told His disciples, "Come away by yourselves to a desolate place and rest a while" (Mark 6:31). In spite of all he had to do, He saw the need to get away and take a break.

IT PAYS TO REST

Let's take Jesus' invitation as our own and seek ways to rest and lighten our loads. Studies have shown that rest is necessary for optimal work effectiveness and healthy well-being. For example, former NASA scientists found that workers returning from vacations demonstrate an 82 percent increase in job performance, with longer vacations making a greater impact than shorter ones.[2] So how can we get more rest (and where's the nearest cruise ship)?

Learn what helps you rest best. Learn to really *relax*. Stretch regularly. Breathe deeply. Scientists have found that our bodies are designed to alternate expending energy and recovering energy called pulsing. This pulsing involves approximately 90 minutes of intense focus, which needs breaks to renew and rewire the brain to focus again. So take a break every hour and a half if you can.[3] Energize yourself with an afternoon nap if it doesn't interrupt your night sleep. Set regular bedtimes and get adequate sleep. Give the day to God in prayer and then rest in His perfect peace (Isaiah 26:3).

Set boundaries. It's wise to understand your limits for your own physical, emotional, and spiritual well-being. Don't feel you must commit to things you don't have the desire, time, or energy to adequately accomplish. It's okay to say *no*. You can respond to requests kindly but firmly by explaining, "I've decided to spend more time with my family, so I'm not committing to anything else now." When you do commit, set timeframes for how long you are willing to serve: "I'll be happy to serve on the committee for the next year." As Larenda Roberts rightly observes, "It is a mistake to agree to take on something until death, doomsday or burnout relieves you of it."[4]

Find some "get-away-girlfriends." Whether it is planned or spur of the moment, getting away with friends can refresh your body and spirit. Just be sure your purpose is not to spend money or impress others but to rest and have a good time. Kidnap a girlfriend for the afternoon and do something you both have always wanted to do. Contact old classmates for a memory-filled reunion. Return refreshed and revitalized. Jesus found the need to get away with His friends and so should we (Mark 6:31).

Learn to work smarter, not harder. Sometimes you may be working harder than necessary. You need to ask yourself, *What can I do to make this job easier?* See if you can delegate some responsibility, find better tools to save time or energy, streamline the process, or even decide not to do the job at all. It's all right to lower your expectations so that you don't demand perfection of yourself. Give yourself permission to let some things go like eliminating the job you dread the most once a month.

Give yourself a breather from challenging situations. A constant barrage from noisy neighbors, loud music, and banging/beeping construction equipment can drain you. So can demanding friends and others who are confrontational, gossiping or meddlesome. Caring for disabled or elderly loved ones can deplete you physically and emotionally. Situations like these can sap your energy so you need to periodically rejuvenate by getting away. Remember that during His ministry, our Savior made time to get away to pray and to spiritually recharge for His mission (Mark 1:32-39).

Redefine "vacation." Vacations don't have to involve a lot of travel, money, and time nor do you have to work a year to earn one. The important thing is to break your routine and do something unusual. Determine what you need at the time, whether it's solitude, activity, rest and/or a change of scenery. There are so many ways to refresh our bodies and souls. Trek the backroads to discover interesting people and places. Make the time to learn how to paint, rock climb, or cook gourmet food. Have the time of your life serving in a mission or humanitarian effort. Enjoy a "second honeymoon" with your mate. Challenge yourself to see how frugal fun can be.

Make a mini escape. Create an idea board or notebook of things to do out of the ordinary when you are short on time. How about "one tank of gas" or "one night" getaways—doing all you can squeeze into those parameters? Experience a mother/ daughter weekend at a retreat or spend quality time with your son learning to play pickleball. Take a family "staycation" by just exploring local attractions you have never visited before. Don't forget to do something special for yourself to rejuvenate.[5]

THE BEST FOR REST

In the Bible the Sabbath served as a symbol of Israel's covenant relationship with God and the spiritual rest He provided while in His care (Exodus 31:12-13). Today, God still offers a Sabbath rest to His people. If we are faithful, Jesus offers us this spiritual rest here (Matthew 11:28-30) and ultimate rest in the hereafter (Revelation 14:13). "So then, there remains a Sabbath rest for the people of God, for whoever has entered God's rest has also rested from his works as God did from his. Let us therefore strive to enter that rest, so that no one may fall by the same sort of disobedience" (Hebrews 4:9-11). Only in the Lord will our souls find true rest. As the psalmist wrote, "For God alone my soul waits in silence; from him comes my salvation" (Psalm 62:1).

ARE WE THERE YET?

1. What advice did Jethro give Moses and why?

2. Why was it wise for Moses to allow the leaders of the tribes to choose the judges from each of their own tribes (Deuteronomy 1:9-13)? What principle can we learn from this today?

3. Why did God rest on the seventh day? How did He make that day special?

4. Why don't Christians observe the Sabbath today (John 20:1)?

5. What did Jesus mean when He said that Sabbath was made for man and not man for the Sabbath (Mark 2:27)?

6. How does God still offer a Sabbath rest to His people (Hebrews 4:9-11)?

7. Why can we as Christian women be prone to overworking?

8. Why do we often feel inadequate when we compare ourselves with the Proverbs 31 woman? How does understanding the premise behind this passage help us?

9. Why does it ultimately pay to rest spiritually, physically, and mentally?

10. What are some opportunities for rest, relaxation, and rejuvenation available to you?

TRIP TIPS: Keep Moving!

The Lord blessed Moses with strength even when he was old (Deuteronomy 34:7). It's a good thing because he needed every bit of vigor to put up with the Israelites. But even Moses grew tired while he lifted his hand in determining victory against the Amalekites. That is when Aaron and Hur stepped in to help keep his hand lifted so the battle would be won (Exodus 17:12-13).

We might not always have friends to help us when we are weary, but we can be proactive to forestall fatigue. Ironically, some of our fatigue comes from sitting still. It's been estimated that 80 percent of American workers sit in front of a computer all day and most hate that aspect of their jobs.[6] Many of us sit at work, sit to drive or ride home, and sit to watch TV after dinner. One report in the *Annals of Internal Medicine* linked sitting that long to increased risk of health problems like cancer, diabetes, dementia, weight gain, and heart disease.[7]

If you feel tethered to your desk at work, break away by going to the furthest copy machine or restroom. If feasible, visit a colleague instead of emailing. Stand and/or pace while you are on the phone. Take the stairs instead of the elevator. Periodically switch hands when you use your mouse and alternate actions (clicking or rolling). Walk for half your lunch hour.

Be mindful to take breaks when working at home. Every so often stretch your muscles to avoid strain. Rotate sides when you carry heavy loads (packages or babies). When you can, reduce the load in half to make it more manageable (laundry). When using repetitive motions (vacuuming, dusting, washing windows), alternate your hands. Take breaks and keep moving!

BAGGAGE CLAIM

"I'm so tired I get winded riding escalators." Phil Callaway

"Most middle-class Americans tend to worship their work, to work at their play, and to play at their worship." Gordon Dahl

"Man is flying too fast for a world that is round. Soon he will catch up with himself in a great rear-end collision, and man will never know that what hit him from behind was man." James Thurber

"There is virtue in work and there is virtue in rest. Use both and overlook neither." Alan Cohen

"The time to relax is when you don't have time for it." Sidney J. Harris

"If you are burning the candle at both ends, you are not as bright as you thought you were." Anonymous

BRING IT ON HOME

What one thing can you do this week to lighten your load by packing more rest into your life? Write it here:

_____

CHAPTER 7

CONTENTMENT
Wanting Just What You Really Need

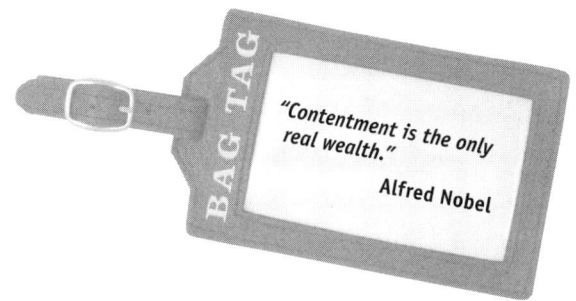

"Contentment is the only real wealth."

Alfred Nobel

Someone has quipped, "Those that say you can't take it with you have never seen a car packed for a vacation trip." Packing light can be a foreign concept when it comes to vacations. Just trying to pack the necessities without forgetting anything can be exasperating, but trying to limit the non-essentials can erupt in mortal warfare.

Then comes the real fun of the trip. "Why couldn't I bring my pet lizard?" "I want to eat now!" "Are we there yet?" And that's just from your husband. Trying to pacify everyone while living in close proximity for several days can wear down the most seasoned traveler. You just hope that someone packed contentment in the mix.

Whether traveling on a vacation trip or the trip of life, it is often difficult to find the state of contentment. In the Old Testament, one man found his way there.

KING ON THE RUN

King David was on a trip, but it wasn't for pleasure. In fact, he was a man on the run for his life. His son, Absalom, had cleverly planned a coup with his own rebel army ready to strike and take over his father's throne. It was a time of intrigue and betrayal.

David and his royal entourage fled out of Jerusalem to the hills, and it was a sad day for the kingdom of Judah (2 Samuel 15:13-18).

David made his way to the town of Mahanaim, and three men from towns nearby brought food and supplies for David and his fellow travelers. Being from the vicinity, these three knew the travelers would be "hungry and weary and thirsty in the wilderness" (2 Samuel 17:29). The three brought a substantial amount of aid for David and his people: bedding, bowls, pottery, wheat, barley, flour, roasted grain, beans, lentils, honey, curds, sheep, and cheese (2 Samuel 17:28-29). These were welcome and generous gifts to the weary group who had left in a hurry with no time to pack.

To engage Absalom and his army, David planned the strategy, but he was considered too valuable by his commanders to lead the charge in battle. Stationed at the gate of the city, he eventually heard the heartbreaking news that Absalom had been killed by the king's own commander, Joab. David was heartsick but headed back to Jerusalem. There he was greeted by Barzillai, one of the three generous men who previously had given him aid when he needed it.

David was so grateful for Barzillai's help in providing for his army in the desert that the king offered to provide for Barzillai the rest of his life, a kind of royal social security. The eighty-year old Barzillai was wealthy but a reward like this was the highest honor, the greatest wealth, and the most secure future that a citizen of the kingdom could be given. Who wouldn't want to live in a palace for the rest of his life?

But Barzillai declined David's invitation. He reasoned that in getting older he might become a burden to David. He was content, choosing to die and be buried in his hometown. He proposed that Kimham (probably his son) accept the king's invitation (2 Samuel 19:37; 1 Kings 2:7). The king agreed, kissed his elderly friend, and blessed him. Barzillai then went home.

RICH IN THINGS THAT MONEY CAN'T BUY

Barzillai could have chosen the royal life at David's court, where he would have enjoyed the king's patronage that few in the kingdom could claim. Instead he was content to go home. Let's look at reasons why Barzillai could be satisfied with his choice and what we can learn.

He knew his priorities. Barzillai had found what meant most to him—to help others, be responsible for himself, and appreciate what he already had. He knew what he possessed was more important to him than living with a king. We need to understand what really matters and then live our lives like we believe it. Start by thinking what possessions you would save if your house were burning down. Most likely they would include family photos and heirlooms. These have little or no monetary value, yet they are priceless and often irreplaceable.

He knew the limitations of age and wealth. Barzillai realized that even a prosperous life in a palace could not ultimately restore his health or youth. Author Phil Callaway reminds us of things money can and cannot buy: "Nice houses, but not a home. A fancy bed, but not a peaceful sleep. Companions, but not friends. Food, but not satisfaction. Sex, but not love. New cars, but not safety. Pills, but not health. Fun, but not fulfillment. Sun-filled vacations, but not peace." [1]

He knew his real home. Though a royal lifestyle might appeal to some people, Barzillai longed for home. For us as Christians, our citizenship is in heaven, and, we should long to go home (Philippians 3:20). As C.S. Lewis wrote, "If we find ourselves with a desire that nothing in this world can satisfy, the most probable explanation is that we were made for another world." Barzillai was wealthy, but that wasn't the source of his contentment. He was content because he possessed things that money can't buy—a generous heart, a humble attitude, and a loving spirit. What a rich man indeed!

OUR DISCONTENT-BREEDING SOCIETY

We live in a rich country with so many opportunities. Yet historian Arthur M. Schlesinger, Jr., has observed that America has been characterized by an "inextinguishable discontent."[2] We have so much, yet we still want more. Even though it was written by Solomon thousands of years ago, Ecclesiastes 5:10-12 accurately portrays the modern emptiness, greed, and anxiety of discontent:

> "Whoever loves money never has money enough; whoever loves wealth is never satisfied with his income. This too is meaningless. As goods increase, so do those who consume them. And what benefit are they to the owners except to feast their eyes on them? The sleep of a laborer is sweet, whether they eat little or much, but as for the rich, their abundance permits them no sleep."

Modern researchers have actually documented this "the more you have, the more you want" phenomenon called "lifestyle creep." They found that when people make more money, they often find extra things they must have like fancier cars, better name brand clothes, and larger homes.[3] Playing the "Comparison Game" soon becomes the norm, and greed becomes part of a three-way cycle with jealousy and envy. As Charles Swindoll wrote, "Greed, jealousy and envy are akin to each other. Greed wants more. Jealousy hoards what it already has. But envy wants to have what someone else possesses." Often this cycle is a desperate attempt to obtain not necessarily the things themselves but the image-driven needs they represent—accolades, affirmation, affection, approval, and acclaim.

We live in a fast-paced, complicated world, full of more choices than mankind has ever known. Modern advances of technology make products outdated before we get them home from the store. Our economy is built on "planned obsolescence," the philosophy that goods are built to fail, wear out, or become less desirable so that consumers will be forced to buy again and again. We are busy, so we value our convenience and time more than our money, and we are willing to pay the price.

The effect of marketing on our buying habits is astounding. Advertising trains us to "need" the new and improved. The constant media blitz on Facebook, Twitter, email, snail mail, radio and the Internet can eventually wear us down. Who can resist an online 50 percent off sale with free shipping that ends at midnight tonight? Apparently few of us can. Allegiance to brand names is another marketing tool that lures us to buy. Whether through a favorite sports team, beloved cartoon character, or top end designer label, branding starts early with exclusive baby products and grows with the child to adulthood.

All these societal factors complicate our journey to the state of contentment and can make it more difficult to find. So how can we find our way? Get ready to learn from someone who has been there—the apostle Paul.

LEARNING CONTENTMENT 101

The apostle Paul made an extraordinary claim in Philippians 4:11-12 about contentment: He could be content in any circumstance. What makes this extraordinary is that Paul was one of the most persecuted followers of God in the Bible. His many sufferings for the Lord were extensive (2 Corinthians 11:23-29). Yet he could say that he had learned contentment through all these experiences. How is that possible?

Understanding the context of Paul's statement gives us insight. The Greek word for "content" in those verses had the idea of being satisfied and sufficient.[4] The Cynic and Stoic philosophers of the Greco-Roman world of that time saw contentment as a total, praiseworthy self-sufficiency without the help of anyone else. But the apostle turned this idea on its head by claiming that his contentment was totally dependent on Christ. Paul could know peace, joy, and satisfaction with whatever life dealt him because he cast himself and his cares on his Lord. His trying circumstances had schooled him in learning what contentment truly was and some principles that could help him—and us—reach that state.

Thank God in all circumstances. Through Christ, Paul found he could genuinely thank God, even find joy, in his circumstances. "Rejoice always; pray without ceasing; give thanks in all circumstances; for this is the will of God in Christ Jesus for you" (1 Thessalonians 5:16-18). The word *all* doesn't give us any wiggle room for being ungrateful. Genuine thankfulness signals to God that we put our complete trust in Him to know what is best for us, even if we don't understand the events of our lives (Romans 8:28). If we develop an attitude of gratitude, we can find joy in even small everyday blessings. To live this out, designate some days as "T Days" (Thankful Days) giving thanks to God and others with no complaining allowed. Strive for everyday to be a T Day.

Avoid stinkin' thinkin' in yourselves and others. Paul admonishes us to take our thoughts captive to make them obedient to Christ (2 Corinthians 10:5). Then we can focus on things that are true, noble, right, pure, lovely, admirable, excellent and praiseworthy (Philippians 4:8). Instead we often dwell on asking ourselves "why?" "what if?" and "how come?" When we catch ourselves doing this, we need to yell, *Stop!* in our minds and switch tracks to positive things. If photos on Facebook or Pinterest trigger envy and jealousy, we need to moderate our social media usage. When media advertising tempts us, we can choose to mute, delete, or pitch it. When braggarts and whiners rob our peace and contentment, we should limit the time we spend with them, if possible.

Be satisfied with less. Paul believed, "But godliness with contentment is great gain. For we brought nothing into the world, and we can take nothing out of it. But if we have food and clothing, we will be content with that" (1 Timothy 6:6-8). Contentment can lighten our loads because we don't have the burden of trying to impress other people. Our basic necessities are really few, even though we often feel it is "necessary" to have the latest, sleekest, or biggest. It is amazing how we could be truly happy with less stuff if we tried. We need to pray that God will open our eyes to enjoy what we already have and learn to share it with others. It would help to ask ourselves, *Do I really need this or do I just want it?* We need to realize *Who* we really need. "Keep your life free from love of money, and be content with what you have, for he has said, 'I will never leave you nor forsake you.' So we confidently say, 'The Lord is my helper; I will not fear. What can man do to me?'" (Hebrews 13:5-6).

Put your hope in God. We say we believe that God will abundantly provide what we need. Why then are we so discontent? Paul urged, "As for the rich in this present age, charge them not to be haughty, nor to set their hopes on the uncertainty of riches, but on God, who richly provides us with everything to enjoy. They are to do good, to be rich in good works, to be generous and ready to share, thus storing up treasure for themselves as a good foundation for the future, so that they may take hold of that which is truly life" (1 Timothy 6:17-19).

THE SEARCH FOR THE GREENER GRASS

Today many people are trying to take hold of life in a different way. They scramble in a relentless, discontented pursuit for the proverbial "greener grass" on the other side of the fence. They are on an endless search for more, bigger, and better things and can't be satisfied. To them, the grass is always greener somewhere else.

But things are not always as they seem. As Phil Callaway writes, "When the grass looks greener on the other side of the fence, the water bill is higher." Discontentment exacts a high price. There are costs involved when people don't seek contentment and instead seek to satisfy their own selfish desires. Whether they are looking for more prestige, a larger house, or a better husband, the seeds of discontent can reap broken hearts, broken homes, and broken relationships. The grass only looks greener because it has "been spray painted by the Deceiver himself. Contentment keeps our eyes on the right side of the fence."[5]

The child of God doesn't need to search for the "green grass" of contentment because the Lord provides it. This is poetically portrayed in Psalm 23 through the imagery of lying down in "green pastures." That familiar psalm attributed to David could be called the "Psalm of Contentment." In it we see the lovely picture of content sheep cared for by the Shepherd with such images as being led beside still waters, comforted through the worst fears of life and death, and anointed with overflowing blessings. Through it all, the psalmist writes, "I shall not want" (Psalm 23:1). With God as our Shepherd, we can be filled and satisfied. Why seek contentment anywhere else?

ARE WE THERE YET?

1. Why did David flee Jerusalem? What did Barzillai and two other men provide for David and his entourage and why?

2. What was Barzillai's reply to David's proposal? What can we learn from him?

3. Why do you think America has been characterized by an "inextinguishable discontent"? How does Ecclesiastes 5:10-12 portray the modern emptiness, greed, and anxiety of this kind of discontentment?

4. What societal factors complicate the Christian's quest for contentment?

5. What extraordinary claim did Paul make in Philippians 4:11-12? What was the Greco-Roman meaning of contentment and how was Paul's claim different?

6. How do you think Paul could find ways to give thanks in all circumstances (1 Thessalonians 5:16-18)? How can we?

7. Why are our thoughts so important in seeking contentment? What are some ways we can avoid "stinkin' thinkin'"?

8. Do you think Paul literally meant that we could be content

with only food and clothing (1 Timothy 6:6-10)? What was his point?

9. Why is it so important to put our hope in God and not in our possessions?

10. What are some ways people search for "greener grass" today? Where can the child of God find "green grass"?

TRIP TIPS: What-to-Wear Contentment

Jesus knew we would be tempted to worry about what to wear (Matthew 6:31). After all, we ask ourselves a lot of questions when we put on an item of clothing, whether we are aware of the self-talk or not.

1. How fashionable is it (cultural)? Is it current and in style?

2. How does it fit (physical)? Does it complement my face and figure?

3. How does it make me feel (psychological)? Do I feel dowdy or attractive?

Clothes are much more than they seem. No wonder we look at our closets in the occasional exasperation of a what-to-wear conundrum. We can find contentment in our closets if we spend some time planning and then leaving the rest to God who will provide what we really need (Matthew 6:28-34).

Find some stores with clothes you like. Learn about sales through their mailing lists. Sometimes department store sales rival discount stores. Keep up with styles to update your wardrobe, if necessary. We don't have to be slaves to fashion, but we don't have to be chained to the '80s either!

Conquer your closet—don't let it conquer you. Weed periodically. Arrange your clothes so you can find outfits quickly (color or type of clothing with hangers facing the same way). Put accessories where you can see them. Rotate your clothes (putting freshly clean clothes to one side), so you can wear all you have. If an item doesn't work for you, pass it on to someone who can enjoy it. Pack up out-of-season clothes, or put them in the far corner of the closet to get them out of your way. Use your clothes to accentuate you, not the other way around.

BAGGAGE CLAIM

"Contentment is an invisible line. It's the line between 'I need' and 'I want.'" Unknown

"There are two ways to get enough. One is to continue to accumulate more and more. The other is to desire less." G.K. Chesterton

"You are content when you can enjoy the scenery along the detour." Unknown

"To know when you have enough is to be rich beyond measure." Lao Tzu

"Be content with what you have but never with what you are." Unknown

"When you complain about your circumstances, half the people who hear aren't interested, and the other half are glad you finally got what's coming to you." Unknown

BRING IT ON HOME

What one thing can you do this week to lighten your load by packing more contentment into your life? Write it here:

_____

WHAT TO UNPACK

Author Glenn Clark observed, "If you wish to travel far and fast, travel light. Take off all your envies, jealousies, unforgiveness, selfishness, and fears." His "ditch list" isn't all we need to leave behind. Any cumbersome dead weight in our bags loads us down and impedes our journey in life. In the next chapters are some things we need to unpack for good.

DEBT
Making Sense of the Dollars

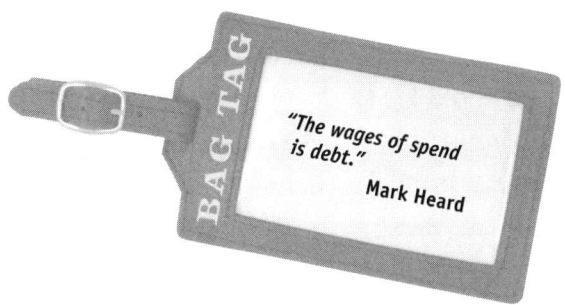

"The wages of spend is debt."

Mark Heard

C ould we really pack for a month in a carry-on suitcase? Apparently it can be done if packing light is done right. Of course, it depends if we are going to an international convention in Geneva or on safari in the African bush. For some of us, the carry-on would just be enough for the first day!

But there are valid reasons why we should pack as little as possible. It makes for a neater suitcase, cheaper baggage fees, easier transport, and more room for trip purchases. When space and weight are at a premium on a trip, we don't want to be limited by our baggage.

The Queen of Sheba had no such baggage limits. When she tested the wisdom of King Solomon with hard questions, her large caravan of camels were packed with spices, precious stones, and 120 talents of gold (1 Kings 10:10). That's 4.5 tons of gold! Packing light was not her strong point.

Solomon's wisdom and wealth exceeded the report she had heard in her country. The Queen of Sheba was overwhelmed not only with his wisdom but also his lavish riches and the extensive burnt offerings in the temple. She wasn't the only royalty to visit Solomon and be impressed by his splendor. "The whole world" sought audience with this Israelite monarch blessed by God who "was greatest in riches and wisdom than all the other kings of the earth" (1 Kings 10:23).

GETTING WISE ON WEALTH

If there is one thing Solomon knew about, it was money. As the richest king of the world at that time, he experienced the height of luxury. He had a lot to say about money in his writings in Proverbs. Solomon still amazes us with his wisdom on wealth in the following proverbs that ring as true today as they did thousands of years ago.

Proverbs 12:11 "Whoever works his land will have plenty of bread, but he who follows worthless pursuits lacks sense." Though we all don't farm our own land now, it still takes work to have something worthwhile. Beware of get-rich-quick schemes. If something sounds too good to be true, it usually is. Check out any business deal thoroughly before you invest.

Proverbs 13:11 "Wealth gained hastily will dwindle, but whoever gathers little by little will increase it." How quickly we can fritter away money and then wonder where it went. The change for that daily coffee or favorite vending machine snack mounts up. However, if we set aside that change, even a few dollars a week can make our savings accounts grow. Paying attention to the details of our spending and saving can make a big difference. Ben Franklin said, "Beware of little expenses. A small leak will sink a great ship."

Proverbs 15:16-17 "Better is a little with the fear of the LORD than great treasure and trouble with it. Better is a dinner of herbs where love is than a fattened ox and hatred with it." If we can cherish loving relationships with God and others, we are rich beyond measure. Millions of dollars could not buy that love. If love is missing in our lives, it doesn't matter how much money we have.

Proverbs 17:16 "Why should a fool have money in hand to buy wisdom, when he has no sense?" Knowing how to handle money is as important now as it was in Solomon's day. When husbands take all the financial responsibility in the family, sometimes their wives are not as knowledgeable as they should be. Whenever you can, take opportunities to learn how to manage your money through your family, friends, books, seminars, and the Internet.

Proverbs 19:17 "Whoever is generous to the poor lends to the LORD, and he will repay him for his deed." This reminds us of Jesus' words "...as you did it to one of the least of these my brothers, you did it to me" (Matthew 25:40). No matter how rich or poor we may feel, there is always someone who has less than us. When we open our hearts to them and give what we have, no matter how large or small the amount, God will bless us (1 Timothy 6:17-19). Some sage has observed, "Money can't buy happiness—unless you spend it on somebody else."

Proverbs 21:17 "Whoever loves pleasure will be a poor man; He who loves wine and olive oil will not be rich." In Bible times, an abundance of wine for drinking and oil for anointing were symbolic of a life of luxury. Today the symbols might be different, but a continual urge to splurge on self-indulgent pleasures can eventually make us poor. Just because some people are lulled into a false sense of financial security by their six-digit salaries does not mean they can't end up bankrupt. Excessive or uncontrolled living above our means will lead to poverty.

Proverbs 22:7 "The rich rules over the poor, and the borrower is the slave of the lender." The Israelite practice of selling themselves or their children into slavery to pay off their debt was a heartbreaking solution to debt and was sometimes abused (Exodus 21:2-7; Nehemiah 5:4-5). Today we still see people "enslaved" by debt. Think of the woman charging to buy whatever her heart desires who finds herself with staggering credit card debt. Plan to pay off debt as soon as you can, and don't let credit card companies "own" you. Thomas Jefferson advised, "Never spend your money before you have it."

Whether we are loaded with money or debt, Solomon's insights challenge us to make some sense of our dollars. Sadly, he did not always follow the advice of the proverbs he wrote and collected. As he grew older and richer, he was drawn further from the Lord and was influenced by his hundreds of foreign wives and concubines to worship idols. He trusted in his wisdom and wealth but not in his God (1 Kings 11:1-6).

A MATTER OF LIFE AND DEBT

Solomon would have been wise to follow the example of his great-great grandmother, Ruth, and her mother-in-law, Naomi. They remained true to God even though they experienced financial feast and famine. They knew how to make it in tough times and when times got better.

Naomi suffered through a famine in her homeland, relocation to Moab, and the death of her husband and two sons in that foreign land. This economic setback left Naomi practically destitute and emotionally devastated. She was so discouraged that she wanted to change her name from Naomi (meaning "pleasant") to Mara (meaning "bitter"). Amazingly, Naomi's daughter-in-law, Ruth, cast her lot with Naomi and all her problems even after Naomi encouraged her to return to her own home in Moab (Ruth 1).

By working together, both women found strength and friendship in meeting the economic challenge to survive. They were victims of circumstances at a time when few provisions were made for widows—no Medicare, life insurance, or Social Security benefits. They could be compared to the homeless in our society. In spite of this, they learned several ways to survive and thrive.

They had a plan. When Naomi heard that there was no more famine in Israel, she was ready to go home to Bethlehem. There she would have the support of friends who believed in her God. When Ruth chose to follow her mother-in-law wherever she went, she also chose to worship Naomi's God. God kept the two unaccompanied women safe on what was undoubtedly a dangerous trip from Moab to Bethlehem. In Bethlehem, Naomi's plan was to sell her husband Elimelech's land to his kinsmen (Ruth 4:3). It was important for land to stay within the family since there was no provision in the Law of Moses to pass inheritance from husband to wife (Leviticus 25:23-28; Numbers 27:1-11; 36:1-12).

They were resourceful. On their arrival Ruth offered to work in the fields. She ended up in the field of Boaz, a relative of Elimelech, and an upstanding member of the community. Naomi proposed a way to let Boaz know of Ruth's availability in marriage through the kinsman-redeemer relationship, and Ruth followed her suggestion.

They worked hard. Naomi tended their home while Ruth worked in the fields. A provision in the Law allowed the poor to follow the men wielding the sickles to harvest any leftover sheaves in bundles for themselves. This made it possible to preserve their dignity without being totally dependent on others (Leviticus 19:9-10; Deuteronomy 24:19-21). Ruth worked steadily day after day and even brought home leftovers for Naomi to eat. Ruth's dedication to her mother-in-law so impressed Boaz that he determined to be Naomi's kinsman-redeemer and eventually married Ruth in the transaction (Leviticus 25:35; Ruth 4:13).

Some people might see the story of Naomi, Ruth, and Boaz as an ancient Cinderella story where all live happily ever after but that misses a much deeper meaning that we can glean. We see the hand of God in each step of their journey—His protection in famine, His provision in plenty, and His progeny in the future. It was through Ruth and Boaz that the future king David came as well as our King, the Lord Jesus Christ. What a gift to all of us! God took some poor women and made them—and us—very rich indeed.

WHEN TIMES ARE TIGHT TODAY

We live in some tight times today. These can be caused by circumstances beyond our control, but they can also be caused by poor financial choices. In the U.S., we live in a debt-ridden society. America is a land of plenty, and it seems about everything costs plenty too. It is estimated that credit card debt in the average American household is more than $15,000.[1] Many Americans live from paycheck to paycheck without any savings or contingency funds. One survey found that only 38 percent of those polled would have enough to cover a $1,000 emergency room visit or $500 car repair.[2] Many people overbuy and undersave. That kind of spending has affected us all—individually and nationally.

So what can we do today to survive and thrive when times are tight? We can translate Naomi's and Ruth's principles to the 21st century.

Have a Plan. Be intentional with your money. Pray for wisdom to utilize a budget. Set aside money for God first. Get organized and know where your assets and important documents are. Keep track of your spending. Use credit cards sparingly and pay them off promptly. If necessary, follow Dave Ramsey's advice to perform "plastic surgery" and cut your credit cards in half. Set thermostats to save energy. Limit your shopping and concentrate on seasonal and clearance sales. Opt for basic plans in telephone and cable service. Reshop insurance for lower payments. Cancel magazines and catalogs that tempt you.

Be Resourceful. Maximize what is available to make your money go further. Find free/cheap entertainment (books from library, picnics in park, matinee movies). Network with others to barter/trade for services, tools, and toys. Ask about child/senior discounts for restaurants, attractions, and motels. Check out thrift stores, flea markets, and yard sales for bargains.

Work Hard. Be willing to do it yourself if you can. Find additional seasonal or temp work to help with expenses. Make extra money at home as a typist, web designer, babysitter, music teacher, language tutor, or seamstress. Pack your lunch and make your morning coffee. Give baked goods, homemade gifts, and service coupons for special occasions. Hold a giant garage sale. Grow, freeze, and/or can your own food. Seek cheaper substitutes for recipes. Learn to do simple clothing repairs.

These ideas might seem simplistic to someone who is floundering in debt. Certainly if you or someone you know needs help, seek knowledgeable experts or friends who can advise you. But don't underestimate how following simple steps like these over a period of time can lighten your financial load, save you money, and help dig you out of debt.

FULL OR EMPTY?

Many people dream of "living the good life" with the latest cars, luxurious homes, exotic vacations, and having whatever they want when they want it. For them, this kind of life would be "as good as it gets." What they often forget is how much money and eventual debt it takes to keep up that type of extravagant lifestyle.

Solomon knew firsthand what it was to live this way "at the top." What did he discover? "All is vanity" (Ecclesiastes 1:2). This older, wiser, rich man was disenchanted with the empty life he had chosen. He concluded that fearing God and doing what He commands should be man's ultimate purpose for living (Ecclesiastes 12:13).

Let's redefine the best kind of life as "a good life"—full, superabundant, brimming with things that money can't buy. Naomi knew this kind of life with Ruth and Boaz. What made the difference? It wasn't the things they owned but the relationships they nurtured. They invested in people. Besides her relationship with God, Naomi's life was full of friends, family, and a precious new grandson Obed whom she might have thought she would never live to see.

We can find the same abundant life in loving God and other people. As Christians, being truly rich doesn't depend on our money in the bank but the love for others in our hearts. As the apostle Paul's admonished: "Owe no one anything, except to love each other, for the one who loves another has fulfilled the law" (Romans 13:8). If we do that, our lives will be overwhelmingly full indeed.

ARE WE THERE YET?

1. Why did the Queen of Sheba visit Solomon? What was her response to what she saw and heard (1 Kings 10:1-13)?
2. When God asked Solomon what he wanted, for what did he ask? Why is it important for us to ask for the same thing (James 1:5-8)?
3. What are some specific examples demonstrating Solomon's wisdom and wealth (1 Kings 3:1-15; 4:22-34)?
4. How would you summarize in a sentence each of Solomon's proverbs cited in this chapter? How can people today use/misuse money in these ways?
5. Who led Solomon away from God (1 Kings 11:1-6)?
6. What are some reasons more people don't have an emergency fund? What is our individual and collective responsibility in the church to help people in times of emergency (Matthew 5:42)?
7. How did Ruth and Naomi use their resources and work hard to make a new life for themselves? How is God's providence evident in their story?
8. What are some ways to survive and thrive today when times are tight?
9. In their later years, why do you think Solomon's life seemed empty and Naomi's life full?
10. In Romans 13:8, did Paul mean we should never buy anything on credit? Within the context, what is the true intent of the passage?

TRIP TIPS: Shopping Savvy for a Real Deal

Among other qualities, the worthy woman in Proverbs 31 was a savvy shopper (Proverbs 31:18). Such an attribute came in handy when she haggled over prices in the marketplace with merchants who might be dishonest (Amos 8:5-8).

Today with a world marketplace, shopping savvy is even more crucial. With 24/7 advertising, hundreds of choices, and the ultra-convenience of shopping on the Internet in your pajamas, it is too easy to spend money. Pray for wisdom every time you shop. Weigh the pros and cons in these tips to see what works best for you. It just depends on your situation.

Shop around to compare quality and prices, *but* consider your time and gas to be sure it is worth the expense. Preview the Internet for a price range.

Good quality items usually cost more and last longer, *but* realize buying a cheaper one might work just as well if quality is not essential for your purpose.

Buy in bulk, *but* be sure you can use up big quantities. Factor in fees for membership-only stores to see if the savings compensate.

Be willing to wait for some items to go on sale at the end of the season, *but* realize that the item you really want might not be available then.

Great deals like "buy one get one free" and "free gift with purchase" sound enticing, *but* don't buy an item you don't need just because the deal sounds good.

Trade in coupons for products you use, *but* calculate the cost and quality of a cheaper generic brand without coupons that might work just as well for you.

Think you are "born to shop"? Remember that you've been "born again"!

BAGGAGE CLAIM

"What you don't owe won't hurt you." Unknown

"A wise person should have money in their head, but not in their heart." Jonathan Swift

"Money was invented so we could know exactly how much we owe." Cullen Hightower

"Some people are always in debt because they keep spending what their friends think they make." Anonymous

"If your outgo is greater than your income, your upkeep will soon be your downfall." Anonymous

"Live like no one else now—so you can live like no one else later." Dave Ramsey

BRING IT ON HOME

What one thing can you do this week to lighten your load by unpacking debt from your life? Write it here:

_____

CHAPTER 9

DISCOURAGEMENT
Being Lifted Out of the Pits

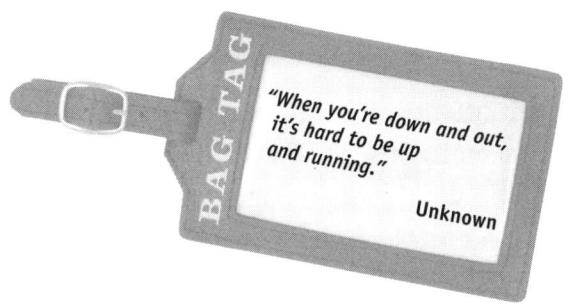

"When you're down and out, it's hard to be up and running."

Unknown

The prophet Elijah knew how to travel first class. What would it have been like to be fed by angels (1 Kings 19:5-8)? What better way to cross a river than to strike it with your cloak and walk on dry land (2 Kings 2:7-8)? How about taking the trip of your life with the Lord providing a whirlwind to take you to heaven (2 Kings 2:11-12). Traveling doesn't get much better than that!

Elijah could pack light because the Lord provided for him with food from ravens and a hair garment with a leather belt (1 Kings 17:5-6; 2 Kings 1:8). Elijah's earthly packing might have been lightweight but he was a "heavyweight" prayer warrior. His fervent prayers impacted thousands in Israel and the surrounding nations. It was the power of God working through those prayers that climaxed in one of the most dramatic contests between good and evil in the Bible. In this confrontation there was no doubt who the winner was. However, soon afterward, Elijah was so discouraged he wanted to die. How could this dynamic prophet land in such a pit of discouragement?

ALMIGHTY GOD VS. BAAL

Elijah had a tough assignment as a new prophet. God called Elijah to confront Ahab and Jezebel. Under the rule of King Ahab, the nation of Israel was in spiritual turmoil. Ahab's wife, Jezebel, a princess of Phoenicia, brought Baal worship with her and instituted it as the national religion. In the process she killed many of God's prophets and imported her own (1 Kings 18:4). Together, Ahab and Jezebel led Israel down the path of idolatry away from the true God.

To get their attention, Elijah prayed earnestly that it would not rain for several years. This was a direct challenge to Baal, a fertility god who supposedly brought forth rain and crops. Israel found itself in a terrible drought that extended to Zarephath, a town between Sidon and Tyre, the home territory of Baal. There God showed His superiority over Baal by providing food for a widow, her son, and Elijah in spite of the drought all around them. When the widow's son died, Elijah prayed and the Lord brought her son back to life. God once again demonstrated His omnipotence over Baal, who was thought to "die" in winter but in spring brought crops, animals, and even people back to life.

Through these miracles God was demonstrating His power even before the showdown on Mt. Carmel began. When the day finally came, it was a spiritual contest that would rival any athletic championship of today, except that the rivals were not evenly matched. On the surface Baal was considered a formidable opponent, a god of fire, storm and lightning with thunderbolts in his hands. But Baal's challenger was the Almighty God who created not only fire and lightning but also heaven and earth.

Elijah told Ahab to summon all Israel to Mt. Carmel to see who was really God. The prophet invited the 850 prophets of Baal and Asherah whom Jezebel sponsored. Before this throng of people, Elijah challenged the prophets of Baal to offer a bull to Baal and he would offer one to God. Elijah stipulated, "and the God who answers by fire—he is God" (1 Kings 18:24). The prophets called on their storm god, frantically shouted from morning to evening, and even slashed themselves with swords and spears until their blood flowed. Elijah taunted the priests by asking if Baal was deep in thought, busy, traveling, or sleeping, all activities that gods were supposed to do. Baal made no response.

Elijah repaired the altar and then asked the people to drench it three times with water. He prayed for the Lord to light the sacrifice. In one dynamic stroke, God ignited fire to burn up the sacrifice, wood, stones, soil, and water in the trench. The people fell prostrate and cried, "The LORD—he is God! The LORD—he is God!" Elijah commanded them to seize the prophets and kill them. He then told Ahab to eat and drink because soon there would be a heavy rain. God accepted Elijah's sacrifice by sending fire, and then He answered his prayers by sending rain.

RUNNING IN VICTORY AND DEFEAT

In an amazing burst of physical strength from God, Elijah ran ahead of Ahab in his chariot the fourteen-mile trek to Jezreel (1 Kings 18:46). That evening when Ahab rehearsed for Jezebel the events of the day, she sent a messenger with a message threatening Elijah's life. His first "Elijah run" had been run in victory but now the second "Elijah run" was run in fear and discouragement to the wilderness.

In a disheartening prayer, Elijah asked the Lord to take his life (1 Kings 19:4). In response, God provided an angel to give him bread and water. Refreshed and strengthened by the food, Elijah traveled forty days and nights until he reached Mount Horeb, another name for Mount Sinai, the same mountain where Moses received God's law. Hiding in a cave there alone, Elijah experienced a rock-shattering wind, an earthquake, and a fire, but God was not in those displays of power for Elijah. It was in God's "gentle whisper" that Elijah knew it was his Lord. Elijah told God how he was the only one left serving Him and that the Israelites wanted to kill him just like they had the other prophets before him.

Elijah was so discouraged about his own plight that he had forgotten how powerful God really was. From a mountaintop spiritual experience, Elijah plunged to a low valley of depression and burnout. He felt a failure. He saw himself as the only prophet left who could bring the people back to God. The prophet thought he was God's last hope, but the Lord reminded him that 7,000 of His followers had not bowed to Baal.

God was still working, and He still had plans for Elijah. The Lord took him where he was to raise him up out of his despondency. Elijah had been wallowing in his misery, but God had a job for him to do—specifically to anoint two kings and to anoint Elisha. Giving Elijah something useful to accomplish helped him refocus his mind and heart and bring him out of his discouragement. God can do the same for us.

WE'VE ALL BEEN THERE

Like Elijah, at some time in our lives, we have all been overcome by discouragement, that feeling of sadness, despair, and lack of confidence. Great men and women of God throughout history have experienced the lows of discouragement. Even Jesus was discouraged when many of His followers ceased to follow Him (John 6:66-68).

Since it is an emotion, discouragement can play games in our hearts and minds. It can skew our perspective. It can fog up our view of reality. It is a ploy the devil uses to bring us down and lose faith in God, doubt ourselves, and give up hope for the future. Satan wants us to think, *God can't handle this* or *I've messed up so badly, nothing can help.* If endless loops of this kind of self-talk keep going round and round in our heads, it can put us on the path to depression and burnout.

Life doesn't always end up "happily ever after." Perhaps we are discouraged by a stale marriage, chronic health problem, or shattered dreams. Sometimes our expectations don't align with reality. What we think should happen doesn't always happen, and we get disappointed. Events that are out of our control catch us off guard. Maybe in the past, we had faith in our ability but somehow we fell short. Perhaps we are afraid we will fail in the future so we hesitate to move ahead. Sometimes we trust people and they let us down. We grow disillusioned with humanity in general.

We need to re-evaluate our expectations. Are we expecting perfection of ourselves or others? No matter how hard we try, we are still human. We will all make mistakes. As Christians, we know the beauty of God's love and grace. We also know how difficult it is for us to live right all the time. How can we expect perfection of others who haven't experienced His love and grace?

When we are discouraged, it helps to go to the root of what caused it. We need to ask ourselves, *Why am I discouraged? Did something or someone else cause my discouragement or am I at fault? Is it caused by something beyond my control? Can I do anything about it now? How can I handle this situation differently in the future? Can I learn something from it?* It helps to realize that good can come out of our disappointments, and we can grow from them.[1]

DON'T GET STUCK IN DISCOURAGEMENT

In your journey through life, you may travel through discouragement but you don't have to live there. How can you avoid getting stuck in the doldrums?

Ask for directions. When discouragement sets in, it is crucial that you pray to God and ask for help. God already knows your difficulties, but pouring out your heart to Him reminds you to trust in His care (Psalm 62:8). Vent your frustrations. If you are seriously discouraged, talk with a trusted friend or Christian counselor who can share her wisdom and experience and help you be more objective.

Check your map or GPS often. Be sure you are on the right road by reading and studying the Bible, your map/GPS to heaven. Is your life aligned with the Word of God or are you trying to go your own way? Memorize and rely on Scriptures that affirm God's care and protection.

Journal your trip. Recording details of your trip makes the difference between a blur of activities and the essence of what really happened. In the same way, remind yourself of the details of your life's journey. Write down your true feelings like David did in the Psalms. Note your discouraging times and also how God blesses you. Revisit it when you need encouragement.

Help a fellow traveler. Serve someone else. Share God's love with them. Focusing on the needs of others gets your mind off of your problems. You come to realize that everyone has problems. It gives you a broader perspective and helps you know that you are not alone.

Stop to rest. It is easy to grow discouraged when you are physically and emotionally exhausted like Elijah. Even though it seems counterproductive, moderate exercise can invigorate you, especially if you go outside. Be sure you are getting enough sleep. Listen to inspirational tapes and music. Do something relaxing and creative. As comedian Eddie Cantor noted, "Slow down and enjoy life. It's not only the scenery you miss by going too fast—you also miss the sense of where you are going and why."

Take the scenic route. A sure ride to gloom and doom is dwelling on the tragic events in the news and the thoughtless people in your daily life. You can't ignore these realities of society, but you don't have to ruminate on them. Make the choice to see the best in people and circumstances. Spend time with positive people who lift you up. Spread joy, optimism and hope to others and your load will seem lighter (Romans 12:12).

Choose the high road. If you are discouraged by unkind criticism, stand up for yourself but don't lash back. Listen to what critics have to say, glean what you can grow from, ignore unjustified criticism, and move on. As Fred Propp, Jr. observed,

"Some people seem to go through life standing at the complaint counter."

Keep going. Often the elements can shut your trip down. Ride out the storm. Don't give up. If you lose your momentum when you get discouraged, start moving forward again. When you are on God's side, you are more than a conqueror (Romans 8:31-39). You have the victory in Jesus Christ (1 Corinthians 15:57)!

RESCUED FROM THE PITS

Discouragement can seem like a dark, cavernous pit. At times it feels so deep we can't climb out. We wonder if anyone or anything can rescue us.

Joseph must have felt desperation like that when his brothers threw him into a dry cistern while they decided on his fate (Genesis 37:23-24). It was his temporary prison until some Midianite traders rode by and bought him as a slave. No wonder Joseph pleaded for his life (Genesis 42:21).

Centuries later, the prophet Jeremiah was also imprisoned by his enemies in a cistern, but this pit had mud in it (Jeremiah 38:6). That quagmire meant sure death either by malnutrition or disease. At that time Jerusalem was besieged by the Babylonians, and prisoners like Jeremiah were the first to be forgotten when the food ran out. Fortunately, an official of King Zedekiah named Ebed-Melech kindly rescued Jeremiah. He even padded the ropes with rags so Jeremiah's trip up from the bottom of the pit was more comfortable.

If both men had been left in their pits, they would have surely died. It was ultimately God who rescued them. It is also God who will rescue us from the pit of discouragement. In a psalm attributed to David, the psalmist uses a graphic description of his pit, whether it was real or metaphorical of his precarious situation. In Hebrew, the word *pit* can refer to the grave or the hereafter, so the psalmist felt he was near death before his rescue.[2]

He drew me up from the pit of Destruction,

out of the miry bog,

and set my feet upon a rock,

making my steps secure.

He put a new song in my mouth,

a song of praise to our God.

Many will see and fear,

and put their trust in the LORD. (Psalm 40:2-3).

We can trust that God who rescued him in his discouragement will rescue us and not leave us in our pits. What a wonderful Savior we have (Micah 7:7)!

ARE WE THERE YET?

1. How did Jezebel influence her husband, Ahab, and the nation of Israel in idolatry? *She worshipped Baal + others followed her -*

2. How did God demonstrate His power over Baal through Elijah before the Mt. Carmel contest? What are some examples of Elijah's prayers? *Food for widow Raised widow son from death*

3. Why do you think fire was a crucial component of the contest? Why was such a dramatic showdown necessary at this time in Israel's history? *b/c Baal was a god of fire*

4. What was different about the "Elijah Runs" to Jezreel and Mount Horeb?

5. How was Elijah's perspective skewed by his discouragement? How did God lift the prophet out of his discouragement? *Spoke to Him in a gentle whisper*

6. What part do unrealistic expectations and events out of our control play in our discouragement? What are some examples of these? *Expect too much from church*

7. What are some healthy ways to handle criticism to avoid discouragement?

8. Why is pouring out our hearts to God so important when we are discouraged? *It feels good to unload*

9. Can a Christian be optimistic and realistic at the same time to overcome discouragement? How does Philippians 4:8 apply? *think on good things*

10. How can dwelling on God's promises in Scripture help to lift us out of discouragement?

TRIP TIPS: Praying Beyond Me and My World

When you are discouraged, it helps to pour out your heart to God. During times like that, it is easy to focus only on your problems like Elijah. One way to get your mind off yourself is to remember others in prayer as well. This opens your heart to needs outside your immediate sphere and puts your problems in perspective. It also reminds you of the hope and peace that God offers the world.

To pray for all people in all situations all the time can be a challenge (Philippians 4:6; 1 Timothy 2:1-2; 1 Thessalonians 5:17)! There are so many needs. Where do you begin? To be more intentional in prayer, list specific needs for a month (28 days). Simplify this by dividing needs into four weekly categories. By adding other needs to your prayer list, you move out of your own sphere in expanding circles from "me and my" with these possibilities:

Week 1. Extended family & friends (conflicts, challenges, sickness, crises, lost).

Week 2. Church family (leaders, staff, spouses, ministries, straying members, sick, shut-ins, mission areas, missionaries, unity, holiness, growth, evangelism).

Week 3. Community & beyond (neighbors, schools, colleges, teachers, military, countries, world leaders, elections, wars, disaster aid, refugees).

Week 4. Issues (abuse, abortion, terrorism, poverty, pornography, euthanasia, marriage, prostitution, religious persecution, race relations, occult, atheism).

Personalize your prayers. Ideas can be written on cards, set as reminders on your computer, or read by the voice reader app on your phone. Thinking about prayers beforehand helps you unload the burden of remembering everything. God only knows how many people will be blessed by your prayers.

BAGGAGE CLAIM

"A man can get discouraged many times but he is not a failure until he begins to blame somebody else and stops trying."
John Burroughs

"There are many ways of going forward, but only one way of standing still." Franklin Roosevelt

"Never deprive someone of hope — it may be all they have."
Unknown

"If you can't fly then run, if you can't run then walk, if you can't walk then crawl, but whatever you do you have to keep moving forward." Martin Luther King, Jr.

"Some see a hopeless end, while others see an endless hope."
Unknown

"There is no pit so deep, that God's love is not deeper still."
Corrie Ten Boom

"Don't be discouraged. It's often the last key in the bunch that opens the lock." Unknown

BRING IT ON HOME

What one thing can you do this week to lighten your load by unpacking discouragement from your life? Write it here:

_____

CHAPTER 10

PROCRASTINATION
Putting It Off for Good

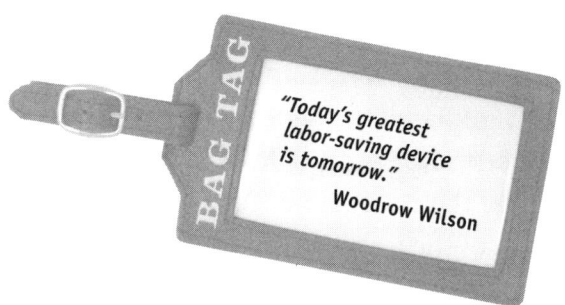

"Today's greatest labor-saving device is tomorrow."

Woodrow Wilson

A ny family who has ever moved themselves knows how over-whelming it is to pack everything they own in a truck and a car (or two)! There are two basic ways to handle this mind-boggling task.

The first is to collect boxes as soon as you can, start systematically packing the lesser-used items in labeled boxes, and gradually count down to moving day. Moving day is still hectic but at least it is controlled pandemonium.

The second is to wait until the evitable can no longer be avoided and start stashing everything in garbage bags and grocery store boxes. Hopefully the lamps won't be smashed, the china broken, and the baby lost in the process.

Whether we are moving or staying put, living in procrastination mode can be disastrous. This is especially true when it comes to accomplishing the Lord's work. Some people procrastinated doing something important for God with long-lasting repercussions.

JUST DO IT—NOW

"Do it now."

King Joash's emphatic command to the priests and the Levites left no doubt as to the urgency and importance of the task—

repairing the temple of the Lord. Solomon's beautiful temple had suffered neglect and defacement through the years, especially since Athalia's sons had broken into it and taken the sacred objects for Baal worship. Baal worship had become the prominent religion during that time, and Joash wanted to make the temple the center of worship to the true God again (2 Chronicles 24:4-5).

Joash was familiar with the temple because it was his secret home for the first seven years of his life. When Athalia took over the throne after the death of her son, Ahaziah, she thought she had murdered all the royal family who might threaten her. But she missed one of her grandsons—Joash. He was hidden in the temple by Jehosheba, sister of Ahaziah and wife of Jehoiada, the chief priest. Jehoiada served as Joash's champion and guide, a relationship that lasted until the priest died. He had put together a clever plan to save Joash and the Davidic line for the kingship. Finally, in a carefully planned coup during the young boy's seventh year, Joash was crowned king over Judah, and Athalia was deposed and put to death (2 Chronicles 22:10-12; 23).

After Joash's coronation, the people made a covenant with God, the king, and the chief priest that they would be the Lord's people. In a spiritual fervor, they tore down the temple of Baal, smashed his idols and altars, and killed his priest. Now the people needed the temple restored to renew worship to God. The temple's place in the spiritual life of the people was crucial to their faithfulness. It served as a powerful symbol of unity where His one people worshiped their one God in one place.

WHAT'S THE HURRY?

So when Joash told the priests to start "now," there was urgency in his commission for this vital task. Yet even in the face of the people's spiritual momentum and Joash's command, the Levites did not act at once. Instead of jumping in with wholehearted dedication, they procrastinated. They delayed making the necessary repairs. Joash questioned Jehoiada and the other priests about why the repairs were not being made. Scripture does not give us the priests' answer to Joash's inquiry, but it sheds light on what might have contributed to their procrastination. Joash told them, "'Take no more money from your treasurers, but hand it over for repairing the temple.' The priests agreed that they would not collect any more money from the people and that they would not repair the temple themselves" (2 Kings 12:7-8).

For whatever reasons, the repair work was not progressing, so Joash devised a different plan. He commanded a chest be set in a visible place in the temple so that the people could contribute for the express purpose of temple repair. The people gave gladly to the project. Soon there was not only enough for repairs but also some extra to make new utensils for the temple. Carpenters, builders, masons, stonecutters, ironworkers, and bronze workers were hired to reconstruct the temple and its furnishings (2 Kings 12:11-12; 2 Chronicles 24:12). The temple became a beehive of activity and finally was being restored.

The refurbishing of the temple was completed, but it took Joash to jumpstart the project. It was the king who urged the priests and Levites to meet procrastination head-on. As spiritual leaders of the nation, they were given an important mission when the temple was in disrepair, and the people were being drawn away by idolatry in the high places (2 Kings 12:3). Their procrastination came at a critical time when the people were teetering between faithfulness and apostasy, which means abandonment of their own beliefs. If their leaders had acted resolutely to restore the temple without delay, the people might have been challenged to be more faithful to God. Sadly, years later Joash and many in the nation of Judah would later revert to idol worship and the Lord's temple would be abandoned (2 Chronicles 24:17-19). The repercussions of procrastination would take a heavy toll on their spirituality for years to come.

MEETING PROCRASTINATION HEAD-ON

Procrastination has been described as a "hardening of the oughteries." We procrastinate when we *ought* to do something, but we are intentionally or habitually slow or late about doing it. Often there are adverse consequences because of our delay.

Delay, however, isn't always bad. There are times when it is prudent to put off or even eliminate an unnecessary or unimportant task. We might be so sick or tired that we should postpone a job and take it easy. It's also wise to take enough time for prayer and advice when making a big decision like marriage or a major purchase. Our Lord delayed His ministry for certain purposes—traveling to the feast in Jerusalem, teaching in the temple, and raising Lazarus to life (John 7:1-10; 14-15; 11:1-6). There were specific reasons for Him to wait.

So postponing action can be good if we have the right purpose. It becomes procrastination when we continue to put off action for the wrong reasons like laziness or fear. If we put off patching the roof, the next rain could leak into our house and ruin our ceilings and furniture (Ecclesiastes 10:18). If we lag behind in paying our bills, we can accrue a late charge. If we keep postponing our doctor's appointment about that lump, it might grow into a malignant tumor. The consequences of our delay can possibly bring damage, debt, and death.

Procrastination can also bring spiritual destruction. We are to reconcile with others as soon as possible to repair fractured relationships and to avoid being taken to court (Matthew 5:23-26). We are not to let our anger fester, but work things out so as not to give the devil a foothold (Ephesians 4:26-27). We should waste no time in sharing the gospel with others, because so many people don't know the Lord (John 4:35). Paul wrote of this urgency, "Behold, now is the favorable time; behold, now is the day of salvation" (2 Corinthians 6:2).

If we procrastinate making our lives right with God, we need to remember that we have no guarantee of tomorrow. James reminds us of life's brevity and uncertainty. Then he adds, "So whoever knows the right thing to do and fails to do it, for him it is sin" (James 4:17). The writer of Hebrews also saw the importance of "today": "But exhort one another every day as long as it is called 'today,' that none of you may be hardened by the deceitfulness of sin'" (Hebrews 3:13).

When the apostle Paul appeared before him, the governor Felix demonstrated how dangerous this kind of procrastination could be. "And as he reasoned about righteousness and self-control and the coming judgment, Felix was alarmed and said, 'Go away for the present. When I get an opportunity I will summon you'" (Acts 24:25). We never read that Felix ever found a convenient time to become a Christian. His procrastination may well have affected his soul's salvation.

WORKING THROUGH THE WHYS

Since procrastination can negatively affect many facets of our lives, it is crucial to learn how we can stop this destructive habit. A valuable first step is to understand why we procrastinate. Discovering why we procrastinate in certain situations can give us insights to overcome it. There can be complex reasons why people intentionally delay in these ways:

Resentment ("I'll get back at her by taking my time to finish this report.")

Fear ("I'm afraid to do it because people might make fun of me if I fail. But if I succeed, they will swamp me with more requests!")

Laziness ("I'm always late for work because I keep hitting the snooze button. Truth is, I really hate my job but I don't want to look for another one.")

Are we more likely to procrastinate in the morning because we are still groggy? Being aware of the times and seasons in our lives can also help us reschedule a better time for an activity. As Solomon wrote, "For everything there is a season, and a time for every matter under heaven" (Ecclesiastes 3:1).

Time of day ~ Are you a morning or an evening person?

Time of month ~ Do you have mood swings and/or low energy levels?

Time of year ~ How busy are the holidays and the start/end of school?

Time of life ~ Are you caring for a young child or elderly/disabled relative?

JUMPSTARTING ACTION

Working through your whys can help you pinpoint the reasons you put off action. Explore the reasons and tips below to help get you jumpstarted for action.

Indecision ("How will I ever choose between this or that one?") Making up your mind can be a real challenge even with incidental decisions. This is compounded because we often have so *many* choices. Pray for wisdom and determine to be more decisive (James 1:5-8). On small decisions realize that the world will not end if you choose a certain outfit or item on the menu. For major ones, take enough time to pray for God's guidance, ask for advice, and investigate for yourself so you can feel you are making the best-informed decision you can.

Perfectionism ("I'll wait until everything is perfect before I try.") If we wait for perfect circumstances or people, we will be waiting a long time. God is perfect; we are not (1 John 1:8-9). Rather, God calls us to strive toward maturity (Philippians 3:12-14). Pray that you will find your significance in Christ, not your performance. Not every task is worth the time, energy, and attention perfectionism requires, so choose where you can best spend yours. You can give yourself permission to be less than perfect. After all, if God offers His grace to us in our imperfection, can we do less?

Drudgery ("I'll put it off because it's too boring/unpleasant.") The best way to tackle many tasks is just to get them completed quickly. But that doesn't mean you can't listen to music or start with the easiest part first to make the job more palatable. Think of how good you'll feel when it's finished when you won't have to worry about it. Reward yourself with something you enjoy when you complete it. If you still make excuses, think of the benefits—like how a clean bathroom is healthier for your family. Even in the most insignificant task, we can find meaning in ultimately serving the Lord (Colossians 3:23).

Disorganization ("This is such a mess—I'll deal with it later.") If you can, find an organized friend who can help you find some order and make it fun. Decide what your purpose (why do this?), plan (what needs to be done?) and process (how is the best way to do it?) should be. Make your goals realistic and commit your plans to the Lord in prayer (Proverbs 16:3). Make a flexible, unstructured schedule and give yourself mini rewards when you make progress. Keep distractions to a minimum to avoid procrastinating. If you get stuck, just tackle something—anything—and soon your momentum will keep you going. [1]

Overwhelm ("I can't handle all this right now so I just won't start.) Even if you are organized, you may feel you can't handle the job because it's too big or you don't have the tools or skill to complete it. Pray for God's guidance and acknowledge you can cast your cares on Him (1 Peter 5:7). Ask for help from family and friends, if feasible. Decide what you want to accomplish, and then prioritize the steps to get there. Break the steps up into doable chunks. "Swiss cheese" the task by taking ten minutes a day to "make holes in it" and cut it down to size. A variation on this is to carve out an hour-blitz each week to focus just on one task and see how much you can get done. Over time, you will be surprised.

IT'S ALWAYS TODAY

One of the most famous procrastinators was Scarlett O'Hara from the book and the movie, *Gone With the Wind*. When she felt she couldn't face something, she rationalized, "I'll think about it tomorrow." She isn't the only one. It has been said that as many as one out of five adults may be chronic procrastinators.[2] Lots of people put a lot of stock in "tomorrow," which ranks up there with "someday" and "later." As H.G. Bohn quipped, "One of these days is none of these days."

The problem is that tomorrow never comes. The big plans we have for tomorrow are often lost in the struggle to juggle our busy lives today. All the things we intended to do but didn't accomplish can haunt us as broken promises, unfinished business, and unfulfilled dreams. We relegate starting a task to "someday." Since "someday" isn't on the calendar, the task is forgotten, and our good intentions never materialize.

Instead of feeling guilty or depressed for past failings, we can determine to see the concepts of now and later, present and future, today and tomorrow in a fresh way. A study published in the *Journal of Consumer Research* found that "today" thinking could motivate us to begin a task and help us view goals in the present rather than the future.[3] An example would be losing weight by creating "now" deadlines (lose two pounds this week) in manageable chunks (two a week instead of 10) with concrete actions steps (start walking three times this week).

Rethinking time can determine if we will complete our tasks and reach our goals or put them off indefinitely. That doesn't mean we will finish everything in the present. It does mean we can start now to take steps to accomplish more than we thought possible, without the extra baggage of procrastination. Instead of Scarlett O'Hara's mode of *thinking* about it tomorrow, we will be *doing* it today.

ARE WE THERE YET?

1. Why is it not always bad to delay taking action? What were some reasons that Jesus delayed in His ministry (John 7:1-10; 14-15; 11:1-6)?

2. How did Jehoiada and his wife, Jehosheba, save Joash's life and the Davidic line of Judean royalty? What happened to Joash's grandmother, Athalia?

3. After Joash's coronation, what did the people of Judah do to show their spiritual fervor?

4. What were Joash's orders concerning the temple to the priests and Levites? What could have been some reasons for their lack of action (2 Kings 12:7-8)?

5. What was Joash's plan to jumpstart the project? What was the outcome of the plan?

6. What are some consequences of procrastination in our daily lives? How can procrastination affect us spiritually?

7. How can the times of our lives affect how we procrastinate? How can awareness of these times help us be more effective?

8. Why is it important to know why we procrastinate?

9. How can indecision, perfectionism, drudgery, disorganization, and overwhelm play a part in procrastination?

10. How significant is the concept of "now" and "today" in the Bible (2 Corinthians 6:2; Hebrews 3:13)? Why is it crucial to think of time in the "present"?

TRIP TIPS: Be Proactive with a HUB

Does any of this sound familiar in the rush of your morning?

"Mommy, I need a costume today. Here are instructions from my teacher."

"Dear, would you please take the car for an oil change this week? I think it's been too long since the last one, but I'm not sure because I lost the receipt."

"I should have called about my aching tooth last week. Has anyone seen the new dentist's number? I had it here on the counter."

One way to communicate better and prevent procrastination is with a Household Ultimate Binder or HUB. Technology is great, but sometimes we need a way to keep information in paper form. This one-stop hub can help keep your home running more smoothly and put information where everybody can find it.

To keep track of papers that need action, assign every family member a file, shelf, or cubby for his or her incoming papers. Process, file, or return those. Then store papers to keep for handy reference in the HUB. Some notebook index topics might include Emergency Procedures, Babysitter Notes, Insurance, Utilities, Recipes, Menu Planning, Shopping Lists, Freezer Inventory, Cleaning Schedules, School Announcements, Class Phone Lists, Chore Lists, Seasonal Checklists, Home and Auto Maintenance, Team Rosters, and Restaurant Menus.

Often you can find free printable template sheets on the Internet for your entries (search "Family Organization Binder"). The notebook format works well for see-through pockets corralling receipts, coupons, and business cards. With the information in one place, you can lighten your paper load and spend your time doing more important things than searching high and low for lost papers.

BAGGAGE CLAIM

"Never put off until tomorrow what you can do the day after tomorrow." Mark Twain

"Nothing is so fatiguing as the eternal hanging on of an uncompleted task." William James

"I do my work at the same time each day, the last minute." Unknown

"When you have to make a choice and don't make it, that in itself is a choice." William James

"The dread of doing a task uses up more time and energy than doing the task itself." Rita Emmett

"Time is free, but it's priceless. You can't own it, but you can use it. You can't keep it, but you can spend it. Once you've lost it, you can never get it back." Harvey Mackay

BRING IT ON HOME

What one thing can you do this week to lighten your load by unpacking procrastination from your life? Write it here:

_____

CHAPTER 11

IDOLATRY
Solving the Case of the Missing God

"There is a God-shaped vacuum in every heart."
Blaise Pascal

Laban was enraged. His household gods were missing. His daughters Leah and Rachel, son-in-law Jacob, plus his 12 grandchildren had packed up their belongings and left his home in a hurry without even saying goodbye. Laban thought they were the likely thieves. He and his relatives took after them in hot pursuit.

Jacob had reasons to be angry with Laban, too. Laban had not only changed Jacob's wages many times, but he had also cheated his daughters, Leah and Rachel, out of their dowry. Jacob's wives agreed to leave their father without a farewell because they felt Laban had "sold" them (Genesis 31:14-16). As for Laban's gods, Jacob knew he hadn't stolen them. How dare Laban accuse him! Jacob declared that anyone found with Laban's stolen gods would die.

Jacob had no idea his wife was smuggling stolen gods. Perhaps she took them to compensate for lost wages and inheritance. These clay or metal figurines were considered religious treasures, possibly family patron gods. They were thought to bring fertility, good fortune, and protection on a journey. They might even have been considered a basis for a family inheritance claim.

After seven days Laban finally caught up with Jacob's entourage.

At Laban's accusations, Jacob invited him to make a search to find his gods. When Laban finally searched Rachel's tent, she slyly pleaded for Laban to excuse her from rising because she was in her period. Little did Laban know that she was hiding the gods in her camel's saddle where she sat. Just the mention of her period would be enough for Laban to search elsewhere. In ancient times a menstruating woman was considered dangerous because her blood was thought to be a host for demons! [1]

We never read of Laban ever solving the mystery of the missing gods, but later Jacob urged his family to do some serious unpacking to get rid of them (Genesis 35:1-5). The family gave him all their gods and the rings in their ears, which might have been amulets with some religious significance. Jacob buried them all under an oak tree in Shechem. At God's call to build an altar and worship only Him in Bethel, Jacob got rid of any gods that might still claim their allegiance.

Hundreds of years later, idols still found their way in the hearts of God's people. For many of these people, there was one God that was missing in their lives. After seeing firsthand the consequences of worshiping false gods, one king sought to find the true one.

THE URGE TO PURGE IDOLS

No doubt people in the kingdom of Judah wondered whom their new eight-year old king Josiah would be like. Would he resemble his father, Amon, who was assassinated by his own officials after a two-year reign? Or would he be like his idolatrous grandfather, Manasseh, who sacrificed his sons in the fire, practiced sorcery and witchcraft, and "...shed very much innocent blood, till he had filled Jerusalem from one end to the another..." (2 Kings 21:16)? Manasseh later repented, but his 55 years as a wicked leader had taken its spiritual toll on Judah.

However, there had to be hope by some that Josiah would be like his great-grandfather, Hezekiah. Hezekiah tore down idols, including the bronze snake Moses had made that some of the people worshiped. He repaired the temple and reinstated worship there after his wicked father, Ahaz, had shut it down. He held a celebration of Passover in Jerusalem so joyous that it was extended seven more days. This spiritual revival prompted the people to destroy the idols in their towns all over Judah. Such an inspirational example might have prompted Josiah, at the age of 16, to seek God.

Josiah cleared the idols. He took worship to God seriously. At 20 he began the most comprehensive purge of idols the nation had ever known (2 Chronicles 34:3-7). He tore down the high places, Asherah poles, carved idols, cast images, and altars to Baal. He made sure they were destroyed and desecrated by breaking them to pieces and then scattering them over the graves of those who had sacrificed to them.

Josiah feared the Word of God. At the age of 26, Josiah commissioned the high priest, Hilkiah, to start overseeing the repair of the temple. In the process Hilkiah found the Book of the Law and sent the secretary, Shaphan, to read it to Josiah. It might have been misplaced or hidden for safekeeping during the long evil reign of Manasseh.

Upon hearing its message (possibly Deuteronomy 28:15-68), Josiah tore his clothes and wept in grief, convicted of the foretold consequences of sin. His fears were confirmed by the prophetess. Huldah, who prophesied that God would bring disaster on Judah because of the evil that Manasseh had done to provoke Him. However, she added that Josiah would not see the disaster because of his humility (2 Kings 22).

Josiah revered the Lord. Josiah conscientiously and systematically began inside Jerusalem and went outward to the far reaches of the kingdom of Judah and even Israel itself to cleanse the land of idolatry. He renewed the covenant with God and the people to serve only God. He also celebrated and centralized the Passover in Jerusalem with the priests officiating (2 Kings 23). The king told the Levites to return to the temple the Ark of the Covenant, probably removed for its protection. (2 Chronicles 35:3).

What was the result of Josiah's exhaustive efforts? "All his days they did not turn away from following the LORD, the God of their fathers" (2 Chronicles 34:33). Sadly, as Jeremiah and other prophets testified, Judah's "following" was external compliance rather than heartfelt commitment (Jeremiah 11:9-13). After Josiah's death, his wicked sons reversed his father's diligent achievements at reform. Because of their idolatry, the nation was eventually led into Babylonian captivity and the horrible events prophesied by the prophets came true.

WORSHIPING MODERN IDOLS

It is hard for us to believe how God's people could be so drawn away by idols that they would prostitute themselves or sacrifice their children on altars just to appease them. We shake our heads at such horrible practices. We think of idolatry as being confined to Old Testament times or pagan cultures throughout history. Basically we see idolatry limited to gods and altars that seem long ago or far away.

However, Paul expands the meaning of idolatry when he relates it to anything belonging to our earthy nature like immorality, impurity, lust, and greed (Ephesians 5:5; Colossians 3:5). Anything we pursue or love in place of God becomes our idol, our ultimate substitute for Him. When we use that definition, we can see that idols are rampant in our culture and in our hearts. People are looking for something missing in their lives, but often they don't know what or who it is. So they seek pleasure in sex. They look for companionship in an affair. They chase after status in wealth. They pursue affirmation in power. But they still come up empty.

Sometimes these gods are hidden like Rachel's smuggled gods. Perhaps a busy executive justifies concealing a bottle in different hiding places to "calm her troubles" when no one is looking. Or a lonely housewife sneaks in yet another erotic bestseller she just can't put down. Or an aspiring entrepreneur takes more cash "under the table" so her business will grow and the IRS won't know.

Other idols might be easier to spot. If we live to eat and eat and eat some more, then food is our god (Philippians 3:19). If we can't miss our favorite show but skip worship instead, TV is our god. If we are wild about our ball team but have no enthusiasm for God, we bow down to the sports god. If we spend more time, money, and energy on looking good than looking to God, we worship the beauty god. If we are so obsessed with playing solitaire on our phones that we neglect our relationship with God, then solitaire trumps God in our hearts.

When we rely on these temporary gods, we ultimately find that they will fail us. When we depend on idols to fulfill us, they will let us down. Like the prophets of Baal in the contest on Mount Carmel, we expect too much of our idols. We take on a heavy burden when we try to prove they are worthy. They will disappoint us because they can't provide what we really need. Isaiah wrote of the uselessness of idols, which also applies to our modern idols: "If one cries to it, it does not answer or save him from his trouble" (Isaiah 46:7).

Only the true God can save us.

Only God can fill our daily needs and the deepest longings in our hearts. Only God can love us so much that He is willing to forgive us when we confess our sins. Only God can know everything about us and still long for a personal relationship with us. God can sustain us when nothing or no one else can. He says, "even to your old age I am he, and to gray hairs I will carry you. I have made, and I will bear; I will carry and will save;" (Isaiah 46:4). What a promise to lighten our loads!

Only the one true God can give us lasting joy and blessing. Our gods may give us a temporary rush, but the feeling doesn't last. Josiah must have observed that emptiness in the unfulfilled citizens of his nation. It prompted him to seek something more in life. No doubt someone in his life influenced him to know God better. As he grew older, Josiah spiritually triumphed in the midst of an idolatrous culture. We can, too.

GETTING TO KNOW THE MISSING GOD

When you want to know people better, you make time to be with them and seek them out. It is the same with getting to know God. We need to seek Him so we can know Him better. We can do this through His Word. The thread that runs from Genesis to Revelation is one of God's love and mankind's redemption. When we seek God through His Word, God shows what He is like by His dealings with mankind.

When Paul visited Athens, he spoke to the people on the Areopagus about knowing the true God. As he walked through the streets of Athens, he was disturbed by all the idols there. He noticed an idol to an unknown god, one who was missing a name. He solved that mystery of the missing god by explaining that it was the God of heaven who created the world and mankind. He was the God who gave them life, breath and everything else. Paul explained, God did this so "that they should seek God, and perhaps feel their way toward him and find him" (Acts 17:27). The implication was that if they sought the true Creator and got to know Him, they would realize how worthless and empty their gods of wood and stone really were.

The same is true with our gods. God wants us to seek Him and know Him up close and personal. Even when we live in a world that worships many physical and spiritual idols, the LORD promises, "But from there you will seek the LORD your God and you will find him, if you search after him with all your heart and with all your soul" (Deuteronomy 4:29).

However, often with our busy schedules we just can't fit God in. He is missing from our lives. Are we so involved in other things that we don't have time for God? "In the pride of his face the wicked does not seek him; all his thoughts are 'There is no

God'" (Psalm 10:4). We need to make seeking God through His Word a priority.

KEEPING OUR APPOINTMENT

To help us to know Him better, God inspired more than 40 writers with different styles over a period of 1,500 years to write His Holy Book. The Bible can help us know what God is like and what He isn't like. What are some things to pack as we read and study His Word?

Purpose. Be intentional in making a time and place for seeking God. Think of it as your appointment with your Creator of the Universe. Keep your Bible, pen, journal, and any other study tools handy so you won't waste time gathering them.

Creativity. Vary your approaches to studying God's Word. Sometimes read the Bible out loud like Josiah did (2 Chronicles 34:30). Utilize a devotional guide like *Power for Today* or *The Daily Bible* with Scripture in chronological order. Find a daily Bible reading schedule you like. Rotate between the Old and New Testaments or read them concurrently. Focus on a book of the Bible and read it daily for 30 days. Take time to savor a verse or read several books quickly to get an overall view. Hone in on a topic or Bible character. [2]

Resourcefulness. Ask your preacher, elders, and Bible teachers what Bible aids they might recommend. Visit Christian bookstores or websites connected with the brotherhood to discover what materials are available to enhance your study like commentaries, word study aids, Bible dictionaries and encyclopedias. If you read religious websites on the Internet, check the source for reliability.

Curiosity. Approach the text with a fresh perspective and ask questions like "why" and "how." Dig for answers about word meanings, biblical customs, and difficult passages. Try to discover what the text meant to the readers then and how to apply its message to us today.

Expectation. Psalm 119 is brimming full of the blessings of God's Word for us if we just "get into" it. The Bible can keep us from sin (v. 11), give us comfort (vv. 76-77), grant us wisdom (vv. 98-100), preserve us (v. 93), and give us joy (v. 111). No other book can do so much for us. May we be able to say with the psalmist, "I delight in your decrees; I will not neglect your word" (v. 16).

JOSIAH'S HERITAGE IN SEEKING GOD

Josiah's commitment to seek God and serve Him throughout his life was exemplary. Josiah's tireless work to tear down the physical idols of his culture serve as an inspiration to those faithful in the nation he ruled. His commitment to God's Word proved that it could achieve a far-reaching purpose for God's people (Isaiah 55:9-11).

J. Barton Payne wrote a tribute to Josiah's lasting influence and how it touches even us today through Jesus Christ:

> Josiah instituted the most thorough of all the OT reforms, dating to 622, and one that restored Israel's commitment to God's book. It was this faith in holy Scripture that was then able to keep the nation's hope alive during the Exile through most of the succeeding century (cf. Da 9:2), during the difficult century of restoration that followed (Ezr 7:10; Mal 4:4), and during the next four hundred silent years until the appearance of John the Baptist (Mal 3:1; 4:5-6) and the kingdom of Jesus the Messiah, God's personal Word, who fulfilled the written Word (Mt 5:17-18).[3]

Through the centuries, men and women have sought to solve the case of the missing god. In a culture of worthless idols, Josiah found the true God through God's Word. May we also find Him. As the psalmist affirms, "Incline my heart to your testimonies, and not to selfish gain! Turn my eyes from looking at worthless things; and give me life in your ways" (Psalm 119:36-37).

ARE WE THERE YET?

1. Why did Jacob want to leave quickly to go back to Canaan? How did his wives feel about the move?

2. Why might Rachel have stolen her father's household gods? Later, what did Jacob do with his family's household gods?

3. What were Josiah's great-grandfather, grandfather, and father like as rulers of Judah? Which one did he follow spiritually?

4. What are some of the ways Josiah purged idolatry in Judah and Israel?

5. What part did repairing the temple play in the spiritual revival of Judah? What are some possible reasons why the Book of the Law was "lost"?

6. In what ways can Josiah's attitude toward God's Word be an example to us today?

7. What are some modern gods that we might worship today? What makes them so appealing?

8. How can we better understand what God is really like by reading and studying His Word? How can this help us be more like Him?

9. What are some different approaches to make our Bible reading/studying more profitable?

10. Why is it important to be intentional about the time we spend with God's Word?

TRIP TIPS: Fixing God's Word in Your Heart

Do you remember some words to the songs you loved as a teen-ager? Maybe you learned them because you heard them over and over again and sang along. You can use a similar process to learn Bible verses. Memorizing Bible verses doesn't have to be boring, difficult, or just for kids. Make it fun!

Start with what you already know like verses you remember from childhood or songs from worship. (Think John 3:16 or the song "The Greatest Commands.") Write them on cards and start a file. Choose verses that speak to you right now. If you don't know where to start, check for lists of verses to memorize on the Internet or from your minister. Learn the reference along with the verse.

Utilize technology by finding memory verse apps for your phone that have fill-in-the-blanks, quizzes, and ways to record the passage so you can play it back. Free websites offer interactive features where you can track your progress. Take a screen shot of a Bible verse on your phone and lock it so you can repeat it every time you see it. Set a reminder on your phone or computer every few hours to say the verse. Texting a verse to friends can reinforce it in your mind.

Maximize your unique learning style by using a visual (seeing), auditory (hearing and listening), or kinesthetic (hands-on) approach. Put cards near your treadmill, sink, or laundry room or in your pocket, lunch bag, or purse. Utilize travel time by listening to CDs of verses or make up your own songs.[4] Draw colorful pictures or cartoons for key words. Use humor and exaggeration to imprint images in your brain. Review them periodically to be sure the verses stay with you. Retrieving a verse when you need it will serve you in so many ways. [5]

BAGGAGE CLAIM

"When we lose God, it is not God who is lost." Unknown

"Nothing is too big for Him to handle and nothing is too small to escape His attention." Jerry Bridges

"Emotion without devotion is nothing more than commotion." Unknown

"Worship is the believer's response of all that he is—mind, emotions, will, and body—to all that God is and says and does." Warren W. Wiersbe

"No one ever truly comes to know, honor, or worship God without being changed in the process." James M. Boice

"We only learn to behave ourselves in the presence of God."
C. S. Lewis

"When it comes to idolatry, the danger is not in an item...it is in us...We are all looking for something to worship and serve. Idols come easy, but go hard." Ed Stetzer

BRING IT ON HOME

What one thing can you do this week to lighten your load by unpacking any idols from your life? Write it here:

CHAPTER 12

WORRY
Trusting God Who Is Always Up

"For peace of mind, resign as general manager of the universe."

Unknown

Not everyone is like Jesus who slept on a rocking boat through a tempestuous storm. Away from home, getting a good night's sleep in a strange place and unfamiliar bed can be an elusive challenge. Even packing a well-beloved pillow cannot always make up for a lumpy mattress, semi-functional air conditioning, or a blaring TV next door. Putting up with less than ideal conditions often makes for a restless night's sleep. Many travelers can't wait to get home to sleep in their own beds.

In the Bible there was a king who had a sleepless night, but it wasn't because he was away from home. What stressed out this king who couldn't sleep? And why was the object of his stress peacefully resting in a lion's den?

SLEEPLESS IN BABYLON

In Daniel 6, King Darius couldn't sleep. In fact, he was so worried about his official, Daniel, that he refused food and entertainment. When a king refuses the possibility of music, dancing girls, and concubines, he is worried! Ever since the 62-year old king of Persia had taken over the Babylonian kingdom at Belshazzar's death, he had organized the new administration with 120 satraps, who were lower-level administrative governors over districts, with three higher (local rulers) officials over them. He was so impressed with Daniel's ability as one of those officials that he planned to set him over the whole kingdom. But a deceitful plan by the other administrators and satraps resulted in the king's being manipulated and Daniel being thrown in the lion's den. Not only had the king lost his key official, but he also had essentially authorized his death.

Perhaps during his sleepless night, Darius thought about how the Judean captive, Daniel, had been blessed by his God. Even in his eighties, Daniel made no secret of his allegiance. He had faithfully served three kings—Nebuchadnezzar, Belshazzar, and now Darius—and had been rewarded for his service with high appointments. But he also faithfully served his God. Darius might have heard about Daniel's refusal to eat the assigned royal food tainted with idolatry and contrary to Jewish purity laws (Daniel 1). The king also might have known about Daniel's ability to interpret dreams to foretell the future of kings and kingdoms (Daniel 2, 4-5). If he was not aware before, Darius knew now that Daniel prayed three times a day to his God with his window open facing Jerusalem (Daniel 6:10).

Darius knew because his other officials had "caught him in the act" of praying, and for this, Daniel was condemned to die. The king might have wondered what their motive was—jealousy, insecurity, prejudice or all three? They had deceived the king into thinking that all the officials had agreed to support the edict they proposed: Anyone caught praying to any other god or man except Darius for the next 30 days would be thrown to the lions. However, Daniel certainly did not concur.

Darius was worried sleepless because it seemed too late to save Daniel. Medo-Persian laws could not be altered. The king and the other officials had sealed Daniel's fate with their signet rings in the hot wax on the stone at the mouth of the den (Daniel 6:17). There was no turning back what devious men had concocted.

THE ONE HOPE OF RESCUE

But wait—perhaps Darius saw one hope of rescue. On the surface, it seemed as if the God of Judah had deserted His people. They were a captive nation in a foreign land. But this God certainly seemed to work in Daniel's life. Could the God whom Daniel served so faithfully rescue him?

At the first light of dawn, Darius hurried to the lion's den to learn of Daniel's fate. He screamed in an anguished voice, "O Daniel, servant of the living God, has your God, whom you serve continually, been able to deliver you from the lions?" (Daniel 6:20).

An eternity must have seemed to pass in time until Darius heard Daniel's voice, "O king, live forever!" Daniel explained that God had sent an angel to shut the mouths of the lions, so they had not hurt him. He also told Darius of his innocence before God and the king.

Darius was overjoyed at the news and gave orders for Daniel to be lifted out of the den. There was no wound on him because he had trusted in God. The accusers' plot boomeranged and Darius had them, their wives, and children thrown in the lions' den. The lions overpowered them and crushed their bones before they hit the floor.

GOD'S PEOPLE NEED NOT WORRY

Darius was so moved by Daniel's rescue that he sent out a decree throughout the land to fear and revere the God of Daniel. In his witness of God's power, this pagan king claimed Daniel's God was the living God who delivers and performs signs and wonders in heaven and on earth. Whether this decree influenced the citizens of Darius' nation is uncertain, but it undoubtedly comforted the exiles there. Through Daniel, God had demonstrated His power and love for His people. He had not abandoned them. They did not need to be afraid.

We see a vivid contrast in Darius' sleepless night. He anxiously carried the burden of what had happened and his part in it. In his pagan culture, Darius knew only distant, capricious, and unpredictable gods who did not care about their devotees. No wonder he had no faith in them to save them.

On the other hand, Daniel could be calm and confident in the true Almighty God even in a lion's den. We don't know if Daniel fell asleep there, but we know he could have. He could have lived this verse: "When you lie down, you will not be afraid; when you lie down, your sleep will be sweet" (Proverbs 3:24). We know he trusted in God, so he didn't need to be afraid or worry. Why worry when he—and we—have such a God? We can enjoy the same peace and confidence that he did.

WHAT—ME WORRY?

Christians certainly have access to God's peace, but do we truly experience it daily? Are we worry-free or do we struggle with anxiety just like people in the world? After all, in our society, worry is considered the norm. Even in Christian circles, it is considered a "respectable sin." We worry about what we have and what we don't have. We worry how long our good relationships will last and why our bad ones didn't. We worry about finding jobs, keeping jobs, losing jobs. We worry when we are well if we will get sick and when we are sick if we will get worse. One worrywart complained to another, "I have so many problems that if anything else happens, it will be a month before I get around to worrying about it."

In Matthew 6:25-34 in His Sermon on the Mount, Jesus didn't accept worry as a necessary part of life. Though His listeners were probably of the poorer class with genuine concerns over food and clothing, the Lord allowed no place for worry in the lives of God's children, whether rich or poor. In verse 31, Jesus' "do not worry" had the idea of "don't even start worrying."[1] Note that Jesus did not call for us to manage or limit worry, but to eliminate it. He saw it not as a casual problem but as a serious issue of trust versus doubt of God's care. The Great Load-Lifter gave us some principles to help us unpack the worry that loads us down. These can help us eliminate this time and energy waster.

Worry is harmful. Why worry when it only hurts us? Jesus reminds us that life is more important than food and the body more important than clothes but we often don't act like it (Matthew 6:25). We work long hours, wearing out our bodies so we can pay for luxuries we don't need and don't have time to enjoy. We are a stressed-out society where many of us suffer from the ill effects of worry. Excessive worry can make us prone to weight gain or loss, heart disease, insomnia, migraines, ulcers, and other physical and mental illnesses. If we find worry interferes with our everyday lives, we need to seek out a Christian counselor or mental-health therapist who can help.

Worry is ineffective. Jesus essentially asked His listeners why they worried about something they could do nothing about—adding a single hour to our life (Matthew 6:27). Yet we get stressed out daily over things we really can't change, like the weather, past events, or other people. The challenge is to do what we can about our problems and then let God do what we can't. As some unknown wit has observed, "If you cannot help worrying, remember that worrying cannot help you either."

Worry is heathenistic. In the Sermon on the Mount, Jesus contrasted what pagans and followers of God pursue in life (Matthew 6:31-33). People who don't know God depend on themselves, and anxiety is a natural response for them. They worry and fret in their pursuit of the necessities of life. But children of God are to pursue the Kingdom of God and His righteousness continually. If we do that, the Lord will take care of all our needs, and we don't have to worry about them. If we worry, we say to God that we think He can save us from the fires of hell, but He can't get us through today.

Worry is wasteful. The things we are worried about might be resolved tomorrow. Why waste time and energy on something that may never happen? As Lucy Maud Montgomery once wrote, "It only seems as if you are doing something when you're worrying." We need to do what we can today and leave tomorrow to the Lord. Each day has enough of its troubles without projecting panic for the future (Matthew 6:34). Instead we should count each day as precious. At the end of the day, we can try to find something we cherished, accomplished, or learned and thank God for His presence and help. We might even find journaling helps us to chronicle the importance in each day.

NOTES FROM PAUL'S WORRY 101

Paul echoed Jesus' message of trust in God's care. If there was a follower of God who could have something to worry about, he did. Take, for example, when he was in prison awaiting trial before Caesar, who would decide whether he would live or die. Instead of a message of fear and anxiety, Paul encouraged his readers to know that "God will supply every need of yours according to his riches in glory in Christ Jesus" (Philippians 4:19). Paul knew God would take care of them and him. He could be content no matter what happened because God was with him and gave him strength (Philippians 4:11-13). He put his life in God's hands and trusted Him for the best outcome. Let's look at some other practical notes from Paul.

Unload your burdens on the Lord. "Do not be anxious about anything, but in every situation, by prayer and petition, with thanksgiving, present your requests to God" (Philippians 4:6). An unknown sage wrote, "The way to worry about nothing is to pray about everything." As soon as you start to feel anxious, pray to the Lord, which is the most powerful thing you can do (James 5:16). Remember the **PRAY** acronym:

P ~ Pour out your heart to God (Psalm 62:8).

R ~ Right now do what you can about the situation (Matthew 5:23-24).

A ~ Acknowledge God's love, power, and care (1 Peter 5:7; Proverbs 3:5-6).

Y ~ Yield to His will, trusting that He will work for your good whatever the outcome (Romans 8:28).

Let God's peace guard your heart. "And the peace of God, which surpasses all understanding, will guard your hearts and your minds in Christ Jesus" (Philippians 4:7). When we pray, God's peace serves as a sentinel to protect our hearts and minds and keep them safe from worry and fear.

Learn from the past and move on. Paul could have agonized over his past mistakes and been tormented with worry and regret. Instead he chose to learn from the past and press on toward his goal—being with his Heavenly Father (Philippians 3:13-14). We, too, should make peace with our past and move on with our lives.

Dwell on the positive. Irritating, upsetting, even tragic events are a part of life, but we don't have to dwell on them. If the apostle Paul had constantly ruminated on his problems, he would have gone crazy. So will we. Instead he urges us to dwell on things that are true, noble, right, pure, lovely, admirable, excellent, and praiseworthy (Philippians 4:8). If these kinds of thoughts pervade our minds, there will be little room for worry. Paul wasn't endorsing a "head in the sand" or "head in the clouds" attitude, but rather a decision to monitor our thoughts and choose the best.

A BATTLE FOR OUR MINDS

Monitoring our thoughts is a key to eliminating worry. Corrie Ten Boom pinpointed it well: "Worry is a cycle of ineffectual thoughts whirling around a center of fear." It thrills Satan when we waste our time and energy in fruitless worry when we could be serving God. The devil wants us to be afraid and doubt that God will do what He says He will do. We are in the thick of a real spiritual battle for our minds (2 Corinthians 10:4-5).

We must identify each worrisome thought and capture it, putting it under control and refusing to let it bushwhack our minds. Then we need to replace it with a more reasonable thought. Let's say we are preparing a presentation. We start worrying, "I will make a mistake and look foolish" (world's thinking). We stop right there and replace it with, "The Lord will help me do this, so relax and do your best" (Christian's thinking). We can only be transformed by this renewing of our minds with the help of the Lord (Romans 12:2).

We also need to differentiate between concern and worry. In his epistles, Paul wrote about a kind of concern that meets a need by caring about others (2 Corinthians 7:7; Philippians 4:10). It realistically focuses on a problem to solve it. This concern is different from worry, which is immobilizing and pointless, keeping people stuck in the muck of the negative "what-ifs" of life. In her book *Letting Go of Worry*, Linda Mintle outlines the difference between worry and concern:

WORRY	CONCERN
Circles the problem	Solves the problem
Brings inaction	Brings action
Feels out of control	Takes control where possible
Distracts from the problem	Focuses on the problem
Disrupts a plan	Puts forth a plan [2]

For example, Stacy lost her job to layoffs in her company. She could have been paralyzed by an unknown future of providing for her two children as a single mother. Dwelling on the uncertain job market, finding a reasonable salary, competing with younger applicants—all these could have immobilized her and brought on panic. However, she chose instead to be proactive about her situation and trust in God. She prayed and asked others to pray for her. She began to update her resume, apply for jobs, and make contacts who could give her leads on job openings. She worked to keep her attitude positive by staying active in her job hunt.

We have a choice just like Stacy. When challenges come in life, we can choose to cave-in to worry or we can trust in God. We can find a unique kind of peace that the world can't offer, a peace that surpasses all our dreams (Philippians 4:7). It's the perfect peace of which Isaiah spoke, "You will keep in perfect peace those whose minds are steadfast, because they trust in you" (Isaiah 26:3). May we be the person who is too busy to worry in the daytime and too sleepy to worry at night.

ARE WE THERE YET?

1. How did Daniel distinguish himself in Babylonian captivity? What lessons can we learn from him as a follower of God in a pagan culture?

2. How did prayer play a role in Daniel's spiritual life?

3. What were the stipulations of the edict the officials proposed to Darius? What could have been the officials' motive(s)?

4. How did God save Daniel? How could Daniel's faith in God's power have influenced Darius?

5. Why do you think some people consider worry a "respectable sin"?

6. How can worry affect us mentally, physically, and spiritually? How can we avoid worry when we face circumstances or people we cannot change?

7. How did Jesus contrast the pursuit of things in the lives of pagans and His followers? How does this relate to worry?

8. Why is it important to focus on today's problems today? What are some ways we can validate the importance of each day?

9. What are some practical ideas from Paul to overcome worry?

10. How does Satan advance worry in the battle of our minds? What is the difference between worry and concern?

TRIP TIPS: The Perfect Insomnia Antidote

Even as Christians, we can experience sleepless nights of tossing and turning. At times, problems related to age and health can prevent us from getting a good night's sleep (as well as noisy neighbors and their barking dogs).

Sometimes sleep eludes us because we can't calm our anxious thoughts or we can't relax because our bodies are so tense. Praying for God's help can help us drift to sleep. Also there are several things we can do to prepare ourselves beforehand like limiting caffeine, learning breathing and stretching exercises to relax, turning down the thermostat and lights, and withdrawing from our "tech toys" an hour before bedtime. The goal should be a calm transition to sleep. Research has shown that sleep makes the last thing we experience become more vivid in our minds. [3] Paul was ahead of his time when he encouraged Christians not to go to bed angry (Ephesians 4:26).

We have God's assurance that we can rest peacefully because He's got it covered. He never sleeps deeply nor even dozes off: "Behold, he who watches over Israel will neither slumber nor sleep" (Psalm 121:4). Like Daniel, the psalmist must have known the security God provides: "In peace I will both lie down and sleep, for you alone, O LORD, make me dwell in safety" (Psalm 4:8) and "I lay down and slept; I woke again, because the LORD sustained me" (Psalm 3:5). It can help to meditate on Scriptures like these to focus on God's protection during the night. Sweet dreams!

BAGGAGE CLAIM

"Never bear more than one kind of trouble at a time. Some people bear three—all they have had, all they have now, and all they expect to have." Edward Everett Hale

"A day of worry is more exhausting than a day of work." John Lubbock

"We would worry less about what others think of us if we realize how seldom they do." Ethel Barrett

"Worry a little bit every day and in a lifetime you will lose a couple of years. If something is wrong, fix it if you can. But train yourself not to worry. Worry never fixes anything." Mary Hemingway

"If you want to test your memory, try to recall what you were worrying about one year ago today." E. Joseph Cossman

"Do not be afraid of tomorrow—God is already there." Unknown

BRING IT ON HOME

What one thing can you do this week to lighten your load by unpacking worry from your life? Write it here:

_____

CHAPTER 13

DISTRACTIONS
Finding Your Focus

"Starve your distractions. Feed your focus."

Unknown

W hat is one of the most distracting things you can do when you are driving? If you said texting on your cell phone, you are right. Studies have found that texting while driving (TWD), or being "intexticated," poses an enormous crash risk, with TWD being around six times more likely to result in an accident than intoxication.[1] Surprisingly, other studies have found that being "lost in thought" can be just as dangerous as fatigue or cellphone chatting. [2] One study showed that daydreaming accounted for 62 percent of fatal crashes involving distracted drivers.[3]

So it's imperative to pack some focus when we drive—or do anything else for that matter. One man of God knew how to keep his focus even in a barrage of distractions.

MAN WITH A MISSION

It was enough to make a man cry. Nehemiah wept when his brother, Hanani, told him of the disrepair of Jerusalem's walls and gates and the "great trouble and disgrace" of the Jewish exiles who had returned to the Judean province (Nehemiah 1:3). These were his people. He felt their shame as it reflected on their God. He felt a shared responsibility for their sin that resulted in Babylonian captivity after Nebuchadnezzar besieged Jerusalem, which now lay in ruins. He felt called to do something about it. So he prayed that God would grant him favor when he spoke to King Artaxerxes of Persia.

As cupbearer in Artaxerxes' court, Nehemiah tasted the king's wine to make sure it had not been poisoned. Such a position held great influence with direct access to the king. Still, Nehemiah was afraid to ask because Artaxerxes had stopped an earlier attempt to restore Jerusalem's city walls. Enemies of the Jews had sent the king false reports, calling it a "rebellious city, troublesome to kings and provinces" (Ezra 4:15). After praying again, Nehemiah courageously asked the king for help in repairing the city. Artaxerxes not only granted Nehemiah permission to go to Jerusalem as governor, but also provided protection on the journey and supplies for the rebuilding effort.

Why were the walls so important that Nehemiah would leave his prestigious position? In ancient times, city walls were a symbol of solidarity and identity. A city with broken-down walls and gates was vulnerable to attack (Proverbs 25:28). It was considered a disgrace to its inhabitants and the entire nation.

But Jerusalem's walls had spiritual implications as well. It was crucial to preserve religious purity that Jerusalem remained separate to prevent intermarriage with foreigners. Walls restricted merchants from selling their wares inside on the Sabbath. Nehemiah saw his task not only to rebuild Jerusalem but also to rebuild a strong spiritual nation from Jerusalem outward. That focus made it imperative for Nehemiah to make the approximate 900-mile journey from Susa to Jerusalem.

After Nehemiah arrived and surveyed the damage, he urged the Jewish leaders to start rebuilding. They agreed. Nehemiah assigned portions of the wall near the workers' homes so they could take ownership in protecting what belonged to them (Nehemiah 3). The Jews in Jerusalem were assisted by citizens from other towns with a variety of occupations—goldsmiths, perfume-makers, merchants, and rulers. Women joined in as well. Some workers worked double duty. What an inspiring example of what could be done when God's people work together under dynamic leadership!

DISTRACTIONS FROM ALL SIDES

However, it wasn't long before the enemies of the Jews were working together to scheme how they could deter progress. They knew if Judah grew strong, their provinces could become weaker. They used different tactics to waste time and divert energy from Nehemiah and the people.

Ridicule—Sanballat the Horonite and Tobiah the Ammonite mocked their efforts. Nehemiah prayed, and the Jews worked with all their heart, building the wall until it reached half its height (Nehemiah 4:6).

Threats—The Arabs, Ammonites, and Ashdodites joined in to threaten Jerusalem. The Jews prayed and posted a 24/7 guard with a trumpeter to sound an alarm, if needed (Nehemiah 4:7-23).

Discouragement—The enemies weren't the only distractors. The workers grew weary from the hard labor, saying, "The strength of the laborers is giving out, and there is so much rubble that we cannot rebuild the wall" (Nehemiah 4:10). Nehemiah encouraged them, and the people kept working from morning until night.

Mistreatment—Poor Jews were being exploited by exorbitant interest rates to the extent of selling their children into slavery. Nehemiah didn't let their valid concerns derail the project but made the guilty Jews give back what they had unjustly taken (Nehemiah 5:1-13).

Harm—Sanballat, Tobiah, and Geshem asked Nehemiah four times to meet them in a village away from Jerusalem. Nehemiah knew they were scheming to harm him and refused (Nehemiah 6:1-4).

Accusation—Next Sanballat sent Nehemiah a letter, accusing him of revolting and proclaiming himself king. Nehemiah prayed and accused Sanballat of just making it up (Nehemiah 6:5-9).

Trickery—Seeking to discredit Nehemiah with the Jews, Tobiah and Sanballat hired the false prophet, Shemaiah, to lure Nehemiah into the temple. This wasn't permitted because Nehemiah wasn't a priest. Nehemiah prayed again regarding those and others trying to bully him (Nehemiah 6:10-14).

Harassment—Tobiah continued to harass Nehemiah with a letter campaign to derail the work (Nehemiah 6:17-19). Through all these distractions, the Jews' enemies were bent on diverting Nehemiah's focus, but he was even more determined to keep on task. As he professed, "I devoted myself to the work on this wall" (Nehemiah 5:16).

DEDICATING MORE THAN THE WALLS

In spite of the demoralizing distractions, the wall was completed in 52 days. When all the enemies heard of this amazing accomplishment, they knew it was with the help of God, and they lost their confidence. It might have seemed like an opportune time to hold a dedication celebration for completion of the walls, but Nehemiah knew his work was not finished.

Nehemiah's ultimate goal was spiritual dedication of the people's hearts. He renewed temple worship by appointing singers and Levites and secured Jerusalem by assigning gatekeepers. With a mass assembly in Jerusalem, the people wept as Ezra read the law and later joyously celebrated the Festival of Booths, which is also known as the Festival of Tabernacles. They confessed their sins and made a written covenant to obey the Lord. This spiritual revival culminated in a dedication ceremony of praise, complete with processions that started at the wall of Jerusalem and ended at the temple.

DRIVEN FROM DISTRACTION?

It seems every time Nehemiah turned around, there was something or someone to divert him from his ultimate focus—to serve God. We have the same challenge. The devil uses distraction to discourage and trip us up. The writer of Hebrews describes two types of spiritual distractions: "every weight, and sin which clings so closely" (Hebrews 12:1). We can understand how entangling sin can hamper our spiritual progress. But anything that gets us sidetracked from our purpose, even if is not bad in itself, can also be a distractor. How can we meet distractions today?

Look to the Lord. Keeping our eyes on the Lord is the only way to keep from being distracted by the enticements of the world. The psalmist wrote, "My eyes are ever toward the LORD, for he will pluck my feet out of the net" (Psalm 25:15). God wants our undivided hearts (Psalm 86:11). Just like anyone who loves us, He is delighted when we seek Him out. We can do that by praying, journaling, reading, and meditating on God's Word. We regularly need to take some time to tune out the outside world so we can intentionally tune into spiritual things. Setting our hearts and minds on things above can help us find purpose and clarity in our Christian walk (Colossians 3:1-3).

Unplug from Technology. An unknown sage once observed, "Wherever you are, be there." "Being there" is a tall order when we are bombarded with tweets, texts, emails, and phone calls we feel we must answer. Add to that the distraction of TV, online games, and Internet shopping. With each new distraction, it takes time to recover the momentum of what we were doing. Distraction breeds more distraction. No wonder we are an increasingly distracted society. Take time to unplug occasionally and take breaks from technology. Create no-tech zones in the house (dinner table, bedrooms) and no-tech times (mealtimes, ride to school, game night).

Mono-Task. It almost seems luxurious, even wasteful, to do one thing at a time when we have so much to do. So we do 50 different things at once and wonder why we feel like crazed banshee women! We soon discover that multitasking is not as efficient and time-saving as it seems. What we are really doing is task switching, toggling back and forth so fast between jobs that it just seems simultaneous. This makes our load heavier. Switching gears actually wastes time and energy because we are never fully absorbed for either activity. Unless tasks are routine and fairly simple, experts have found it is better to mono-task and batch our jobs, concentrating on one thing at a time. An example of this is to chunk one nagging task once a week for one hour in a productive "power hour."

Concentrate on people. Have you ever been at a restaurant and seen a couple or family all looking at their phones instead of one another? What does that say about who is important? In your interactions with people, focus on them (just don't stare!). Don't worry about what *you* will say next but really listen so you can follow-up with comments or questions about *them*. Celebrate any happy occasion with them. Linger at mealtimes for conversation. You will be amazed how focusing on people will enrich your life as well.

WHAT REALLY COUNTS?

What is your focus in life? Where are your priorities? Your schedule reflects what is really important to you. Do your priorities determine your schedule or does your schedule determine your priorities? If you understand God's will for your life, then you can better define your priorities. Romans 12:2 states that Christians can test and approve what God's will is. To do this you need to search God's Word, pray for guidance, and try to get a clearer vision of God's plan for your life (Proverbs 16:3). You can define your priorities by taking time to think intentionally about these questions:

- *What can I do that no one else can?* There are some things that only you are in a position to do (like Nehemiah spearheading the rebuilding of the walls). Developing your faith in God and taking care of yourself and your family would be some of your unique responsibilities.

- *What am I doing that someone else could or should do?* Are you doing something for which you are not really suited (like David planning to build the temple)? Sometimes knowing what you should not do helps you know what you should do.

- *What gifts has God given me? How am I using them?* Do you have skills or abilities you know you do well? Perhaps you also have talents that are hidden or unused that are waiting to be tapped for God's kingdom. Ask family and friends about what talents they see in you.

- *What dream or passion do I have?* Is there something that you have always wanted to do but you never took the time or effort to pursue?

- *What have you been called to do?* How can God use you right where you are "for such a time as this" (like Esther saving the Jews)? When God has a task for you, He will help you accomplish it. [4]

Working through the answers to these questions can help you better know what God wants you to do. It will give you an idea of how He can best use you in the kingdom as an instrument "for honorable use, set apart as holy, useful to the master of the house, ready for every good work" (2 Timothy 2:21).

FOCUSING ON JERUSALEM

Nehemiah felt that he was God's instrument to serve Him in Jerusalem. After he had finished his mission, he left Jerusalem to go back to Susa. He returned 12 years later to find some in Judah had reverted to their old sinful ways. Tobiah had taken over a room in the temple. The Sabbath was being desecrated. The

Jews had intermarried with their foreign neighbors. Nehemiah took action against the law-breakers and tried to restore their spiritual focus.

This sad return to disobedience vividly shows how the Old Testament Jews were unable to fully meet the requirements of the law. A new covenant was needed which only a perfect sacrifice could bring. For this reason God sent Jesus into the world. Like Nehemiah, it is toward the city of Jerusalem that Jesus focused: "When the days drew near for him to be taken up, he set his face to go to Jerusalem" (Luke 9:51). Referencing the "Servant of the Lord" whom scholars think refers to Jesus, Isaiah wrote, "I gave my back to those who strike, and my cheeks to those who pull out my beard; I hid not my face from disgrace and spitting. But the LORD GOD helps me; therefore I have not been disgraced; Therefore I have set my face like a flint, and I know that I shall not be put to shame" (Isaiah 50:6-7).

Jesus knew what lay ahead for Him in Jerusalem. Still He "set [his] face like a flint" toward His task to fulfill the Law and obey His Father's will through His death on the cross (Hebrews 10:5-10). But death could not deter Him from his goal—to rise from the grave (Luke 13:32). "...looking to Jesus, the founder and perfecter of our faith, who for the joy that was set before him endured the cross, despising the shame, and is seated at the right hand of the throne of God" (Hebrews 12:2). We eagerly anticipate seeing Jesus face-to-face in our home in heaven, where we will never need to pack again!

ARE WE THERE YET?

1. Why were the walls and gates of Jerusalem so important to the Jews? How did they provide some spiritual protection as well?

2. How did Nehemiah's organization of rebuilding the walls help them focus on their goal?

3. What were some of the tactics their enemies used to distract the Jews? How did Nehemiah's enemies meet their distractions?

4. What are some examples of the encouragement Nehemiah gave the people to help them refocus on the work? Why did the Jews' enemies lose their confidence?

5. On his return trip from Susa, what spiritual problems did Nehemiah find among the Jews? What did he do to restore their spiritual focus?

6. Why is it so difficult to focus in today's culture?

7. What are two types of hindrances described in Hebrews 12:1 that distract us from doing God's will?

8. What are some examples of distractions that can trip us? What can help us refocus to meet these distractions?

9. What was Jesus' purpose in setting out resolutely for Jerusalem (Luke 9:51)?

10. How can setting priorities in our lives give us more focus in serving God? Why is it important to periodically re-evaluate our priorities?

TRIP TIPS: Can We Exist Without a List?

Did you notice how many lists were in the book of Nehemiah? The lists of genealogies were especially important to the Jews because of their genealogy and inheritance rights (Nehemiah 7:4-73). The lists, in a sense, told them who they were and from where they had come.

Today, lists can tell you where you are going, like action steps to reach your goals. They can lighten your load by helping you focus on your priorities.

Goals List ~ Brainstorm some goals that are important to you. Assuming that God is *the* priority that touches every facet of your life, think of goals in simple categories like Self, Family, Church, Work, and World (or create your own). Narrow your goals to a few, and concentrate only on those for now. For example, you might write a goal for the Family, "Make the family room a more homey place for the family to gather, talk, and play."

Project or Master List ~ Start a running long-term master list of projects with general to-dos like "declutter the family room." Add anything that needs to be done, no matter how large or small the project. Designate a place like a clipboard or legal pad for paper lists or a computer/smartphone for digital lists.

Daily Action List ~ From the master list, limit daily to-do lists to specific actions you can take like "Buy basket for magazines" and "Weed old magazine issues." Take five minutes to set priorities to focus on for the day. You can prioritize by number, alphabet, time involved, and location. In the evening, review your daily to-do list and carry over what you didn't complete to the next day's list. Crossing off what you have done gives you a visual sense of accomplishment!

BAGGAGE CLAIM

"If you chase two rabbits, both will escape." Unknown

"Work is hard. Distractions are plentiful. And time is short." Adam Hochschild

"Do whatever you do intensely." Robert Henri

"You can't do big things if you're distracted by small things." Unknown

"Distraction is a lot like water: first refreshing, then exhausting, and finally, fatal." Unknown

"The question is not "how can I do more?" but "am I doing the right thing?" Jean Fleming

"You got to be careful if you don't know where you're going, because you might not get there." Yogi Berra

BRING IT ON HOME

What one thing can you do this week to lighten your load by unpacking distraction from your life? Write it here:

_____

PACKING IT IN
Activities to Enhance Your Study

1. To visually get a clearer idea of the sequence of Old Testament events in the chapters, make a timeline on the wall or paper. Start with Abraham and Lot in Chapter 3, then Joseph in Chapter 4, and forward all the way to Nehemiah in Chapter 13. It is even better if you can find approximate dates to give an idea of the span of events. This will help you see where the Old Testament characters in the study fit chronologically in relation to one another.

2. Think how some of the characters in the study could have linearly impacted the ones after them, not only in genealogy, but also in their faith or lack of it. For example, how did the grace of Abraham not only impact Lot but also those who followed him? How did Lot's lack of faith impact his daughters and eventually impact Ruth (hint: Moab)? How did her life impact David? How did David's life impact Solomon?

3. For more of a challenge, map the connections among the characters in the Bible stories in a web pattern. Some of these connections might be beyond the stories in this study. Discover how they relate to those before and after them. If possible, find a Scripture to show this connection. For example, you can show a connection between Abraham and Jesus. When the Jews boasted of being Abraham's children, Jesus answered, "Before Abraham was, I AM" (John 8:58). Another example would be when the crowds whom Jesus fed thought he was the prophet prophesied by Moses (Deuteronomy 18:15, 18-19; John 6:14; Acts 3:22).

4. In a class setting, celebrate the culmination of this study by enjoying a meal together. If you are feeling creative, wrap little boxes with brown paper like suitcases to fill with goodies to serve as favors. You can write your favorite Bible verses from the study on your favor to remind you to pack light.

ENDNOTES

Chapter 1 - Enough!

1. Quoted in Jon Mooallem, "The Self-Storage Self," September 2, 2009. *New York Times Magazine: http://www.nytimes.com/2009/09/06/magazine/06self-storage-t.html?_r=0* (December 30, 2015).
2. Mooallem.
3. Mooallem.
4. Arianne Cohen, "No More Clutter," *Woman's Day* (April, 2011), 54.
5. Spiros Zodhiates, ed., *The Complete Word Study Dictionary: New Testament* (Chattanooga: AMG, 1992), 1151.
6. William Barclay, *The Gospel of Matthew, Volume 2, rev. ed.*, The Daily Study Bible Series (Philadelphia: Westminster Press, 1975), 17.
7. Zodhiates, *The Complete Word Study Dictionary: New Testament*, 1482.
8. Barclay, Matthew, Vol. 2, 18.
9. Dawn Dwyer, *How to De-Junk Your Life* (Shawnee Mission, Kans.: National Press Publications, 1998), 47.

Chapter 2 - Order

1. Marilyn Paul, *It's Hard to Make a Difference If You Can't Find Your Keys: The Seven-Step Path to Becoming Truly Organized* (New York: Penguin Books, 2003).
2. Lisa Gibbons and Bill Rancic, "Is Clutter Draining Your Cash?" April 16, 2014. *American Now, News You Can Really Use: http://www.americanownews.com/story/19033948/garage-organization* (December 30, 2015).
3. Kathy Waddill, *The Organizing Sourcebook* (Chicago: Contemporary Books, 2001), 13, 15-16.

Chapter 3 - Grace

1. Richard Blackaby, *Putting a Face on Grace* (Sisters, Ore.: Multnomah, 2005), 43.
2. Blackaby, 32.
3. Elizabeth Scott, "How to Forgive," Last updated December 16, 2014. *About Health: http://stress.about.com/od/relationships/a/how_to_forgive.htm* (December 26, 2015).
4. Scarlett Lewis, "I Forgave My Son's Killer," *Family Circle* (December 2013), 30.

Chapter 4 - Patience

1. John T. Willis, *Genesis*, Living Word Commentary, 2 (Abilene, ACU Press, 1984), 385.
2. Katie Brazelton and Shelley Leith, *Character Makeover: 40 Days with a Life Coach to Create the Best You* (Grand Rapids: Zondervan, 2008), 180-181.
3. Jane McWhorter, *Special Delivery: A Course in Letter-Writing* (Huntsville: Publishing Designs, 2004).

Chapter 5 - Resourcefulness

1. "World War II Rationing on the U.S. Homefront," *Ames Historical Society: http://www.ameshistory.org/ exhibits/events/rationing.htm* (December 27, 2015).

2. Wikipedia contributors, "United States Home Front during World War II." Last updated December 8, 2015. *Wikipedia, The Free Encyclopedia: https://en.wikipedia.org/wiki/United_States_home_front_during_World_War_II* (December 27, 2015).

3. "Municipal Solid Waste," *Wastes-Non-Hazardous Waste-Municipal Solid Waste.* Last updated June 25, 2015. *U.S. Environmental Protection Agency. http://www3.epa.gov/epawaste/nonhaz/municipal/* (November 26, 2015).

4. "How Do I Recycle? Common Recyclables," Last updated November 16, 2015. *EPA United States Environmental Protection Agency: http://www.epa.gov/ recycle/how-do-i-recycle-common-recyclables* (November 26, 2015).

Chapter 6 - Rest

1. Brigid Schulte, *Overwhelmed: Work, Love, and Play When No One Has the Time* (New York: Farrar, Straus and Giroux, 2014), 48.

2. Bryce Covert, "Taking a Vacation May Actually Save Your Career: Workaholism is Hurting the American Economy." June 23, 2014. *New Republic: https://newrepublic.com/article/118285/workaholism-america-hurting-economy* (October 11, 2014).

3. Schulte, *Overwhelmed*, 266-267.

4. Larenda Roberts, "10 Easy Ways to Simplify Your Life," *Christian Woman* (September/October 2006), 16.

5. Tim Hansel, *When I Relax I Feel Guilty* (Elgin, Ill.: Life-Journey Books, 1979), 96, 110-137.

6. Deborah Kotz, "10 Ways Companies Can Encourage Workers to Move," November 3, 2014. *Bostonglobe.com: https://www.bostonglobe.com/lifestyle/health-wellness/2014/11/03/ways-companies-can-encourage-workers-move/BO5BRPZPLBNsEfw3eFS2mM/ story.html* (December 7, 2014).

7. Julie Corliss, "Too Much Sitting Linked to Heart Disease, Diabetes, Premature Death," *Harvard Health Blog.* January 22, 2015. *Harvard Health Publications, Harvard Medical School: http://www.health.harvard.edu/blog/much-sitting-linked-heart-disease-diabetes-premature-death-201501227618* (March 4, 2016).

Chapter 7 - Contentment

1. Phil Callaway, *Making Life Rich Without Any Money* (Eugene, Ore.: Harvest House, 1998), 132.

2. Quoted in Richard Swenson, *Margin: How to Create the Emotional, Physical, Financial and Time Reserves You Need* (Colorado Springs: NavPress, 1992), 186.

3. Sandy M. Fernandez, "Money: Stay on Top of Your Savings," *Woman's Day* (January 2015), 91.

4. Zodhiates, *The Complete Word Study Dictionary: New Testament*, 291, 1479.

5. Swenson, *Margin*, 199.

Chapter 8 - Debt

1. Richard Davies, "Survey Finds Many Americans 'on the Edge of Financial Disaster,'" February 23, 2015. *ABC News: http://abcnews.go.com/blogs/ business/2015/02/survey-finds-many-americans-on-the-edge-of-financial-disaster/* (December 30, 2015).

2. Eric Morath, "Most Americans Don't Have Savings to Pay Unexpected Bill" January 7, 2015. *The Wall Street Journal: http://blogs.wsj.com/economics/2015/01/07/most-americans-dont-have-savings-to-pay-unexpected-bill/* (December 30, 2015).

Chapter 9 - Discouragement

1. Tim Clinton and Ron Hawkins, *The Quick-Reference Guide to Biblical Counseling: Personal and Emotional Issues* (Grand Rapids: Baker Books, 2009), 80-84.

2. H. C. Leupold, *Exposition of the Psalms* (Grand Rapids: Baker Book House, 1959), 323.

Chapter 10 - Procrastination

1. "Understanding and Overcoming Procrastination." Last updated April 4, 2012. *McGraw Center for Teaching and Learning, Princeton University: https://www.princeton.edu/mcgraw/library/for-students/avoiding-procrastination/* (December 30, 2015).

2. Catherine Clifford, "15 Ways to Overcome Procrastination and Get Stuff Done." December 6, 2014. *Entrepreneur.com: http://www.entrepreneur.com / article/240262* (December 30, 2015).

3. Amy Morin, "Study: The Secret To Ending Procrastination Is Changing The Way You Think About Deadlines." September 4, 2014. *Forbes.com: http://www.forbes.com/sites/amymorin/2014/09/04/study-the-secret-to-ending-procrastination-is-changing-the-way-you-think-about-deadlines/* (December 30, 2015).

Chapter 11 - Idolatry

1. John H. Walton, Victor H. Matthews, and Mark W. Chavalas, eds., *The IVP Bible Background Commentary: Old Testament* (Downers Grove: InterVarsity Press, 2000), 64.

2. Nancy Leigh DeMoss, *A Place of Quiet Rest: Finding Intimacy with God Through a Daily Devotional Life* (Chicago: Moody, 2000), 170-172.

3. Kenneth L. Barker and John Kohlenberger III, eds., *Zondervan NIV Commentary, Volume 1: Old Testament* (Grand Rapids: Zondervan, 1994), 673.

4. Andy Rau, "Ten Tips for Memorizing Bible Verses." March 13, 2013. *Bible Gateway Blog: https://www.biblegateway.com/blog/2013/03/ten-tips-for-memorizing-bible-verses/* (October 13, 2013).

5. Stephen Simpson, "How to Memorize Scripture: Tricks and Ideas," *How to Memorize Scripture: http://www.memoryverses.org/tricks.htm* (October 14, 2013).

Chapter 12 - Worry

1. Leon Morris, *Expository Reflections on the Gospel of John* (Grand Rapids: Baker Book House, 1988), 160.

2. Linda Mintle, *Letting Go of Worry* (Eugene, Ore. Harvest House, 2011), 21.

3. Jennifer King Lindley, "While You Were Sleeping...," *Real Simple* (August 2014), 111.

Chapter 13 – Distractions (p. 170)

1. Christina Bramlet, "10 Deadliest Driving Distractions" April 11, 2013. *PropertyCasualty360: http://www.propertycasualty360.com/2013/04/11/10-deadliest-driving-distractions* (November 6, 2015).

2. "Health News: Don't Think and Drive," *Good Housekeeping* (August 2013), 71.

3. William Hampton, "Just How Dangerous is Daydreaming While Driving?" September 17, 2013. *PM: http://www.popularmechanics.com/cars/how-to/a9378/just-how-dangerous-is-daydreaming-while-driving-15935216/* (November 6, 2015).

4. Glynnis Whitwer, *I Used to Be So Organized: Help for Reclaiming Order and Peace* (Abilene, Tex.: Leafwood, 2011), 70-73.